humble effort with
my Special Regards.
Abbas
Aug. 23, 07

Shīʿa Sects

(*Kitāb Firaq al-Shīʿa*)

Abū Muḥammad al-Ḥasan ibn
Mūsā Al-Nawbakhtī

Shīʿa Sects

(*Kitāb Firaq al-Shīʿa*)

*Translated, introduced
and annotated by*

Abbas K. Kadhim

ICAS Press

British Library Cataloguing-in-Publication Data
A catalogue record for this book is available from the British Library

ISBN 978-1-904063-26-1 (pb)

Cover Design by Tarrahan-e Farda

This edition first published in 2007

Published by
ICAS Press
133 High Road, Willesden, London NW10 2SW

Telephone 0044 208 451 9993
Fax 0044 208 451 9994

www.islamic-college.ac.uk

Contents

To Medīḥa
with love and pride…

Translator's Foreword

To a large extent, the knowledge regarding the doctrines of the Shīʿa is generally derived from four well-known scholars whose published work is easily accessible. These in chronological order are al-Ashʿarī (d. 330/935), al-Baghdādī (d. 429/1037), Ibn Ḥazm (d. 456/ 1054), and al-Shahrastānī (d. 548/1153).[1] Of these al-Shahrastānī and al-Ashʿarī are the best known, because their works were published early. All of these scholars are dedicated Sunnis, committed to the idea that the Shīʿa (they often call them the *rawāfiḍ*) are nothing but erroneous heretics. al-Baghdādī presents this view in very clear and unequivocal terms:

If the [person's] heresy is similar to the heresies of the Muʿtazila, the Khawārij, **the Rāfiḍa – Imāmīyya or Zay-**

1 Watt, W. Montgomery, *Islamic Philosophy and Theology*, p. xiii. The author refers to al-Nawbakhtī's book, The Sects of the Shīʿa, as a "partial heresiograph[y]...usually ascribed to an-Nawbakhtī."

dīyya – the Najjārīyya, the Jahmīyya, the Ḍirārīyya, or the Mujassima, he is part of the Muslim community (*ummah*) with respect to some rules, like the permissibility of his burial in Muslim cemeteries, and not depriving him of his share of the booty if he rides with the Muslims, and not forbidding him from praying in the mosques. He, however, is not part of the Muslim community with respect to other rules: it is not permissible to pray behind him or to pray [the funeral prayer] for his body, it is not permissible to eat any meat he has slaughtered, it is not permissible for him to marry a Sunni woman, and the Sunni [man] is not permitted to marry a woman from them if she holds their beliefs.[1]

With views like these, it is impossible for them to fairly portray the Shīʿite point of view. For this reason, it is imperative for serious research to take into account the works of Shīʿite scholars. Two of these are well known to scholars in this discipline. One of them is *al-Munyah wa-l-Amal* by Aḥmad b. Yaḥyā b. al-Murtaḍā (d. 840/1437). This work represents the Zaydite point of view, which is also frowned upon by the four Sunni scholars. However, it is the least attacked among all Shīʿite groups, in spite of being considered heretical. The reason behind this benevolence is often clearly stated; the late Zaydites do not charge Abū Bakr and ʿUmar of any wrongdoing or dispute the legitimacy of their caliphate. Al-Baghdādī, for instance, describes the doctrines of Sulaymān b. Jarīr al-Zaydī, who was a Zaydite chief, and then says that the Sunnis consider him a blasphemer because he accused ʿUthmān b. ʿAffān of blasphemy.[2] He then describes the

1 Al-Baghdādī. *Al-Farq bayn al-Firaq*, p. 14.

2 Ibid., p. 33.

Butrīyya (another Zaydite sect) as a "better" sect, in the opinion of the Sunnis, than the followers of Sulaymān b. Jarīr, because they neither criticized ʿUthmān, nor did they praise him. But their fellow Zadites, the Jārūdīyya, consider them heretical because they do not consider Abū Bakr and ʿUmar to be blasphemers.[1]

The second book is *Kitāb Firaq al-Shīʿa* or *The Sects of the Shīʿa* by al-Nawbakhtī, Abū Muḥammad al-Ḥasan b. Mūsā b. al-Ḥasan b. Muḥammed b. al-ʿAbbās b. Ismāʿīl b. Abī Sahl b. Nawbakht. Al-Najāshī said the following about him: "Our shaykh, the Mutakallim, who surpassed his contemporaries – before the year three hundred [A.H.] and thereafter." He went on to list over forty works by him.[2] Al-Ṭūsī also described him as a pious Imāmī, who was visited by some translators of philosophy books, like Abū ʿUthmān al-Dimashqī, Isḥāq [b. Ḥunayn], and Thābit [b. Qurrah].[3]

In addition to the prestige of its author, *Kitāb Firaq al-Shīʿa* is extremely important for two main reasons. First, it is the earliest work on the subject that has come down to us in its entirety. The second reason has to do with the perspective of the book. It is the only book that provides a Shi'ite point of view on the differences among the Islamic sects and their origins. Since the German scholar, Hellmut Ritter, published the fist edition of the book in 1931, the book became one of the classics in the field and was cited virtually by every author who has ac-

1 Ibid., pp. 33-34.

2 *Rijāl*, p. 179-82.

3 *Fihrist*, p. 75.

cess to Arabic. It was translated into several languages, namely Persian, Urdu, French, and Russian. We now present the first – and long overdue – English translation of this momentous book.

Abbas K. Kadhim
Berkeley
October 10, 2006

Acknowledgements

I feel indebted to many people: to Professor Hamid Algar of the University of California, Berkeley, for his encouragement, for reading the manuscript, and for providing me with many valuable suggestions; to the publishers and editors at ICAS; to the authors of the Persian, French, and Russian translations; and, of course, my everlasting gratitude to my wife and children, Ali and Huda, for their sacrifice and patience for nights too many to count, as I was working on this project.

Translator's Introduction

The primary doctrine of Islam is unity, under the guidance of Allah's ordinances and the rightful rulers. Divergence and dissension are forbidden emphatically. The Qur'ānic verse, "And hold firmly, all together, to the rope which Allah (stretches out for you), and be not divided among yourselves; and remember Allah's favor on you, for you were enemies and He joined your hearts in love, so that by his Grace you became brethren"[1], contains a command that Muslims be united and, for more emphasis, it is followed by a prohibition of division and rivalry. Then, it describes the progress that has been made by the transition from pre-Islamic *Jāhilīyya* to Islam. It was a transition from animosity and malice to brotherhood and love. The catalyst for that was Allah's Grace. To maintain this harmony, there must be another catalyst: total obedience to religious and political authority, which was equated with, and derived from, the obedience to the Divine: "O Believers! Obey Allah and obey the Messenger and those charged with authority among you; if you have dispute about anything, refer it to Allah and the Messenger, if you believe in Allah and the Last Day; that is best

1 Qur'ān, 3:103.

and most suitable for a final interpretation."[1] The Qur'ān mandates total obedience to the source of authority, Allah, and the holders of authority, the Prophet and other legitimate rulers (*Uli al-Amr*). Yet, in the event of a dispute, Allah and the Prophet are the final arbiters. The rulers are omitted to deny them any role in a final arbitration. It is also inferred that the rulers are included in the mandate to refer to Allah and the Prophet, just like the ruled are mandated to do so.

These verses were read selectively and given many twisted interpretations when illegitimate rulers began to ascend to authority. Naturally, they did not struggle in finding scholars of religion, who were willing to endorse such selective and convenient interpretations. Some of them even volunteered to fabricate supportive statements and attribute them to the Prophet himself to preempt any foreseeable objections. The concept of unity was given the status of absoluteness – often at the expense of the reason for unity. The adherence to this concept became the equivalent of faith, whereas any dissent was considered a form of heresy that can be treated only by shedding the blood of those who espouse it. This mandatory status of unity also came at the expense of the congruent conditions of the verse: unity around what? The "Rope" metaphor was forgotten altogether in later readings. Hence,

1 Ibid., 4:59.

unity under oppression was regarded higher than the dissent and strife for justice.

Ibn Khaldūn, in his *Muqaddima*, quotes the jurist and judge of Al-Andalus, Abū Bakr b. al-ʿArabī Al-Mālikī, who wrote in his book, *Al-ʿAwāṣim wa Al-Qawāṣim*, that "al-Ḥusayn [b. ʿAlī b. Abī Ṭālib] was killed according to the law (*sharʿ*) of his grandfather, [the Prophet]."[1] The premise for this historical judgment was built on a statement attributed to the Prophet, that "if anyone wants to divide this united community (*Ummah*), strike him with the sword without regard to his identity." The logic of Ibn al-ʿArabī was the following:

> Anyone who wants to divide the Ummah deserves to be killed.
> Al-Ḥusayn wanted to divide the Ummah.
> Al-Ḥusayn deserved to be killed.

While the smell of fabrication is quite obvious in the statement that was attributed to the Prophet, even accepting it as an authentic tradition (*ḥadīth*) prompts us to read it reasonably. The statement was probably fabricated to serve unjust rulers, by condemning the continuous disenchantment and militant dissent. But even in its form, the statement cannot be read without careful evaluation of "unity" and "division." The spirit of the statement calls for banning malicious division when the Ummah is united on the first principles of its existence, love and brotherhood. Otherwise, common sense imposes the necessity of dividing an Ummah, which is united under oppression and injustice, because such division would create at least one faction that calls for justice and reform.

---

1 *Muqaddima*, p. 217.

To be sure, Ibn Khaldūn mildly points out the mistake of Ibn al-ʿArabī. But was Ibn al-ʿArabī oblivious of this reasoning, as Ibn Khaldūn suggested? Of course he was not. But his attitude is understood only when we remember that he worked for the rulers of al-Andalus, who were a branch of the Umayyad dynasty that was responsible for the killing of Al-Ḥusayn, among many other atrocities. As for Ibn Khaldūn, who was writing in a different milieu, he simply found a middle position that leaves everyone happy, but not our intelligence. For him, Yazīd was a debauchee (*fāsiq*), but no one had the right to fight against him; and al-Ḥusayn was a martyr – he was wrong when he fought against Yazīd, but it was only a temporal error and not a religious error. As to those, who did not support al-Ḥusayn, Ibn Khaldūn says that they were right as well, because they elected to avoid bloodshed and chaos.[1]

Ibn Khaldūn and Ibn al-ʿArabī are only two examples of the literal reading of the Qurʿān and ḥadīth that pays minimal or no attention to the spirit of the text or, often times, even to its authenticity. Their literal emphasis on obedience negates the essence of the concept. The Qurʿānic verse mandates obedience to Allah first, then to the Prophet, and finally to the rulers. The three are listed in a prioritizing manner, but the literal reading has made them equal. The new understanding is that obedience to Allah and the Prophet was vested in the rulers after the death of the Prophet. This reading paved the way for the final step, which represents total neglect of the authority of Allah and the Prophet. The focus was ultimately

1 Ibid.

shifted to the obedience of the rulers. Al-Nawbakhtī narrates an interesting remark about this phenomenon. First, he describes the unity of his opponents as the "unity in giving loyalty to whoever seizes the power over them, whether he is honest or a debauchee. Therefore, their name, "the *Jamā'a*," does not refer to unity of religion." He also refers to the shift of loyalty among the rulers. It only indicates the falsehood of such loyalty. When Abū al-ʿAbbās Al-Saffāḥ died, his successor, and brother, Abū Jaʿfar al-Manṣūr changed the former's designation of ʿĪsā b. Mūsā for the caliphate after al-Manṣūr. Instead, al-Manṣūr designated his own son. When the followers of Abū al-ʿAbbās were asked about the reason for their acquiescence, they replied: "Obedience to the imām is mandatory so long as he is alive. Once he dies and another takes his place, the new imām's order is mandatory as long as he lives."

In the same selectivity, the scholars of *Firaq* dealt with the ḥadīth of the Prophet about the division of the Ummah into seventy-three sects. This ḥadīth became the point of departure for many of these scholars, and the basis for their methodology. The first chapter in al-Baghdādī's work on the *Firaq*, for example, is devoted to this ḥadīth and its application for studying and classifying the Muslim sects. He narrates the ḥadīth according to three different chains of transmission and, interestingly, in three different forms. This difference is not merely an innocuous discrepancy. Here are the three texts, as they were recorded by al-Baghdādī:[1]

"The Jews were divided into seventy-one sects, the Christians were divided into seventy-two sects, and my Ummah will be divided into seventy-three sects."

---

1 *Al-Farq bayna al-Firaq*, pp. 4-7.

"My Ummah will undergo what the sons of Israel went through; they were divided into seventy-two sects, and my Ummah will be divided into seventy three sects – one more sect over what they had – all of them [will end up] in the Fire, except for one sect. They said, 'O Messenger of Allah! Which sect will prevail?' He said: What I – and my Companions – believe in."

The sons of Israel were divided into seventy-one sects and my Ummah will be divided into seventy-two sects; all of them [will end up] in the Fire except for one, the *Jamāʿa*."

The first glance at the three texts shows some important differences between the first version and the other two. The first discrepancy is the omission of the Christian sects in the last two versions. This omission led to another major inconsistency in the numbers of the sects. The Jews had to be seventy-two sects (one more sect than in the first ḥadīth), in order to keep the number of Muslim sects at seventy-three (one sect more than the Jews). The three texts also provide two possibilities of the Muslim division: seventy-three in the first two accounts, and seventy-two in the third.

Another significant difference has to do with the fate of the groups. The first version makes no clear judgment. It can be inferred that the division is not portrayed as the right thing to do – since it is spoken of in comparison with the other religious divisions. But it is not clear how grave the offense of division is and what punishment is prepared for it. The last two texts specifically address this point. All are destined for the Fire, except for one sect. But even there, we can notice a discrepancy. The surviving sect is identified in different ways; once as the one that follows the Prophet and his companions, and another time as the "Jamāʿa." The result from these inconsistencies is that we cannot accept all, or even two, of the three versions as a reconcilable group. The only way is to accept only one and disregard the others. But which version can we endorse?

A survey of the opinions given by the scholars of *Firaq* turns an inconclusive outcome. First, because these opinions range from complete ignorance of the ḥadīth or rejection of its authenticity, on the one hand, to full adherence to all of the three versions, on the other. While al-Baghdādī's book revolves around the ḥadīth, as we have seen, Ibn Ḥazm dismisses the ḥadīth completely, on the basis of the chain of transmission, which he considers to be untrustworthy.[1] Al-Nawbakhtī and al-Ashʿarī omit the ḥadīth altogether, whereas al-Rāzī noticed that he counted more than seventy-three sects in his book, *Iʿtiqādāt Firaq al-Muslimīn wa al-Mushrikīn*, so he re-interpreted the ḥadīth to justify his over-counting:

It is possible that his intent, peace and praise be upon him, was to mention the major sects. Some of what we have counted here are not major sects. Also, he foretold that they will be seventy-three, therefore, they cannot be less than that. Should they be more, it would not be harmful. Why not? For we have not mentioned many famous sects in this brief [work]. It would possibly be many times more if we mentioned all of them. Indeed, we may find seventy-three groups in one of the rawāfiḍ sects – the Imāmīyya.[2]

1 Ibn Ḥazm. *Al-Faṣl fi al-Milal wa al-Niḥal*, vol. III, p. 248.

2 Al-Rāzī, Fakhr ad-Dīn. *Iʿtiqādāt Firaq al-Muslimīn wa al-Mushrikīn*, p. 117.

What Constitutes a "Sect"?

There seems to be a consensus among the scholars of Firaq on the criteria that were used to distinguish the main sects of Islam. Al-Nawbakhtī, al-Ashʿarī, and al-Baghdādī present identical classification of Muslims into four major sects: Shīʿa, Muʿtazila, Murjiʾa, and Khawārij (al-Baghdādī adds the word *Qadarīyya* to the Muʿtazila). Ibn Hazm later kept the same major sects, but he added a fifth one – Ahl al-Sunnah. The same can be said about al-Shahrastānī, who tried to encompass all of the classifications of his predecessors. The only major difference we see in the late writings is the addition of the Ṣufī sect by al-Rāzī (d. 606/1212).

The basis of distinguishing between the major sects does not seem systematic if examined carefully. The minor sects that constitute the Shīʿa are those who advocated the right of Imām ʿAlī to be the successor of the Prophet and the imāmate of ʿAlī's sons – al-Ḥasan and al-Ḥusayn after him – but they differ in almost everything else. The Muʿtazila groups are united around pure theological arguments, beginning with their own five "pillars of religion": God's Unity, His justice, the certainty of fulfillment of His promise and threat, the intermediate position of the grave sinner – between belief and disbelief; and the mandatory nature of enjoining good and forbidding evil. The Murjiʾa are united on reserving judgment on the position of grave sinners. They also endorsed ALL the companions of the Prophet and refused to comment on their disputes, considering all of them to be co-equal in worthiness and validity of judgment. As for the Khawārij, they are united on considering the third caliph,

ʿUthmān, a blasphemer and illegitimate caliph during the last six years of his life. They also agree with each other on considering the grave sinner to be blasphemous. The Ahl al-Sunnah are united on the belief in the creation of man's actions by Allah, Who can torment or reward anyone without regard to their deeds.

The real arbitrariness, however, is encountered upon going into the sub-divisions in each major sect. This arbitrariness may be attributed mainly to the fact that some of the scholars felt that they had to be in full adherence to the ḥadīth regarding the seventy-three sects. Even al-Nawbakhtī, who did not mention the ḥadīth, managed to have seventy-three sects. Was this a coincidence? We may never know.

To take the sects of the Shīʿa as an example, we find that al-Ashʿarī divides the Shīʿa into three major sects, each one branches into many minor sects (Ghulāt, Rāfiḍa, and Zaydīyya). The Ghulāt has twelve minor sects (Bayānīyya, Janāḥīyya, Ḥarbīyya, Mughīrīyya, Manṣūrīyya, Khaṭṭābīyya, two unnamed sects, Shurayʿīyya, Numayrīyya, Sabaʾīyya, and another unnamed sect). The Rāfiḍa has fifteen minor sects (Qaṭʿīyya, Kaysānīyya, Mughīrīyya, Rāfiḍa [I], Rāfiḍa Ḥusaynīyya, Rāfiḍa Muḥammadīyya, Nāwūsīyya, Rāfiḍa [II], Qarāmiṭa, Mubārakīyya, Sumayṭīyya, ʿAmmārīyya/Faṭḥīyya, Wāqifa/Mamṭūra, and two other Rāfiḍa sects). And the Zaydīyya has six minor sects (Jārūdīyya, Sulaymānīyya, Butrīyya, Nuʿaymīyya, Zaydīyya, and Yaʿqūbīyya). The minor sects also branch out occasionally. The Khaṭṭābīyya – a minor Ghulāt sect – has five sub-sects (Khaṭṭābīyya, Muʿammarīyya, Buzayghīyya, ʿUmayrīyya, and Mufaḍḍalīyya); whereas the Kaysānīyya – a minor Rāfiḍa sect – has ten sub-sects (Kaysānīyya I; Kaysānīyya II; Kaysānīyya III; Kaysānīyya IV; Kaysānīyya V, (there is no Kaysānīyya VI) Kaysānīyya

VII; three sects under Kaysānīyya VIII, Rāwandīyya, Razāmīyya, and Abū Muslimīyya; Ḥarbīyya; Bayānīyya; and Kaysānīyya XI). The Jārūdīyya – a minor sect of the Zaydīyya – is also divided into five sub-sects (Jārūdīyya I, Jārūdīyya II, Jārūdīyya III, Jārūdīyya A, Jārūdīyya B, and Jārūdīyya C). The differences among the sub-sects range from substantial differences on the imāmate to very minor opinions, such as their differing opinions about the third caliph, ʿUthmān.

Al-Baghdādī has the Shīʿa in four major sects (Zaydīyya, Kaysānīyya, Imāmīyya, and Ghulāt). He lists the same Zaydīyya sects and sub-sects in al-Ashʿarī, with the omission of the Nuʿaymīyya and the Zaydīyya sub-sects. He also lists the Kaysānīyya as a separate major Shīʿite sect without any minor sects. As to the Ghulāt, he also lists the exact same number of minor sects, but he names the ones that al-Ashʿarī left unnamed (Ghurābīyya, Mufawwaḍīyya, and Dhimmīyya). The Imāmīyya minor sects are listed as fifteen sects without sub-sects, as in al-Ashʿarī, but with differences in names (Kāmilīyya, Muḥammadīyya, Bāqirīyya, Nāwūsīyya, Shumayṭīyya, ʿAmmārīyya, Ismāʿīlīyya, Mubārakīyya, Mūsawīyya, Qaṭʿīyya, Ithnā-ʿAsharīyya, Hishāmīyya, Zurārīyya, Yūnusīyya, and Shayṭānīyya.)

Al-Shahrastānī adopts the major sects of al-Baghdādī sects (Zaydīyya, Kaysānīyya, Imāmīyya, and Ghulāt), but he differs in enumerating the minor sects. For him, the Kaysānīyya are five minor sects (Mukhtārīyya, Hāshimīyya, Ḥārithīyya, Bayānīyya, and Razāmīyya). He lists three Zaydīyya minor sects (Jārūdīyya, Sulaymānīyya, and Ṣāliḥīyya/Butrīyya). The Imāmīyya are listed in a completely different way (Bāqirīyya and Jaʿfarīyya, Nāwūsīyya, Afṭaḥīyya, Shumayṭīyya, Mūsawīyya and Mufaḍḍalīyya, Ismāʿīlīyya, Ithnā-ʿAsharīyya.) Then he lists eleven sects after Imām al-Ḥasan al-ʿAskarī – almost in the same way they are described by al-Nawbakhtī, who mentions fourteen sects with much more detail. The Ghulāt are listed in eight minor sects (Sabaʾīyya, Kāmilīyya, ʿAlbāʾīyya, Mughīrīyya, Manṣūrīyya, Khaṭṭābīyya, Kayyālīyya, and Hishāmīyya). He differs with al-Baghdādī on the status of the Kāmilīyya and the Hishāmīyya, by considering them to be among the Ghulāt.

A Thematic Analysis of *Kitāb Firaq al-Shīʿa*

Al-Nawbakhtī introduces his book with one short paragraph that identifies the problem and his goal. The problem is the dispute among all the community (*ummah*) – Shīʿa and others – concerning the imāmate. This dispute started, he notes, since the death of the Prophet, peace be upon him, and his family, and continued until al-Nawbakhtī's own time. The goal of the book is restricted to recording what was known, in his time, about the disputants and their doctrines on this particular theme; although he alludes at times to other relevant doctrines. Al-Nawbakhtī's exclusive interest in this theme is not arbitrary. It echoes a consensus among other Muslim scholars that was articulated by al-Shahrastānī, who maintained that "the greatest dispute within the *ummah* is the dispute over the imamate, for the sword was not waved, at any time, over any particular religious doctrine more than it was waved over the imāmate."[1] The focus is also justified because the imāmate is one of only a few doctrines about which the Shīʿa diverge from all other Muslims without exception.

The next pages are dedicated to the roots of the dispute and the identity of the first disputants. The death of the Prophet created a political vacuum that immediately produced its offshoots in the form of three parties: the party of ʿAlī b. Abī Ṭālib, the cousin and son-in-law of the Prophet; the party of the *Anṣār*, or the supporters of the Prophet; and the party of Abū Bakr. Each party laid the claim for the validity of its interpretation of political legitimacy. The *Anṣār* depended on their favor in supporting the new religion and offering a refuge for the Prophet and his followers when no one else would lend any help. They also viewed themselves more eligible to rule in their own town (Medīna) than the Migrants. The party of Abū Bakr advanced the claim that the imāmate is not to be given to other than the tribe of Quraysh. Quraysh, they said, is the only tribe that could be accepted by everyone to rule over the rest of Arabia. It is also the tree of which the Prophet is a branch. The party of ʿAlī based their claim on qualifications, the designation of ʿAlī by the Prophet, and ʿAlī's blood relation to the Prophet. When the dust settled, Abū Bakr was appointed as the first successor of the Prophet. After that historical point al-Nawbakhtī very briefly goes over some very important events that transpired during the next twenty-five years that witnessed the rule of three men, namely Abū Bakr, ʿUmar, and ʿUthmān. Of these events,

1 Al-Shahrastānī. *Al-Milal wal-Niḥal*, p. 13.

he mentions the fate of Saʿd b. ʿUbādah, the head of the *Anṣār* party and their candidate, the tumults of certain Arab tribes and their challenge to Abū Bakr, and the killing of ʿUthmān. No details are given on any of these historical milestones. It is also noteworthy to mention that al-Nawbakhtī does not refute any of the arguments he reported. The only reservation he makes is on the story that was given for the death of Saʿd b. ʿUbādah – that he was killed by the Jinns. Al-Nawbakhtī comments on this claim saying: "This, of course, calls for some thinking, for it is not customary that the Jinns shoot arrows at humans and kill them."

The tenure of Imam ʿAlī is given a relatively longer discussion, with some accounts of those who stood aside and the ones who fought against him: the people of the Camel, the Khawārij, and the party of Muʿāwiyah, the governor of Syria. The latter group ended up with the political power after the assassination of Imām ʿAlī, and they were divided in four sects that would make the Murjiʾa. Al-Nawbakhtī continues to give accounts of the Murjiʾa, the Khawārij, and the Muʿtazila and their views concerning the major disputes of the early Umayyad rule. He first relates their doctrines on the imāmate, then the questions about the events that took place during the time of Imām ʿAlī, mainly the status of those who fought against him and each group's position regarding his acceptance of an arbitration between him and Muʿāwiyah. At the end of this discussion, al-Nawbakhtī hints at his opinion about all these groups and their self-description as "the people of unity", saying: "They accuse each other of being sinful regarding [their beliefs] about the imāmate, jurisprudence, religious decrees, and the doctrine of God's unity, among other religious sciences. They refute one another and accuse one another of being blasphemous. Yet, the most notable thing about them is their description of themselves as "the *Jamāʿa*" (united community). They probably refer to their *unity* in giving loyalty to whoever seizes the power over them, whether he is honest or a debauchee. Therefore, their name, "the *Jamāʿa*," does not refer to unity of religion. Indeed, their true condition is that of unequivocal divergence."

At this juncture, al-Nawbakhtī concludes that "all sects are falling under four major sects: the Shīʿa, the Muʿtazila, the Murjiʾa, and the Khawārij." The rest of the book is devoted exclusively to the sects that make together what is generally known as the Shīʿa.

The organization of the book from this point on follows two main necessities. First, there is the timeline of the emergence of every group; and, second, the organization according to mutually shared doctrines. The timeline is important because it reveals the history of each group and its political and social context. It is also important because it allows the reader to trace each emerging group to its original sect. To trace any one of the more recent sects, one has to go back from secondary branches to main branches and end up finally with the main trunk of the sectarian tree. The reason being that the Shīʿa began with one major group that was identified in contradistinction to the other three major groups, namely, the Muʿtazila, the Khawārij, and the Murjiʾa. Then it was divided on itself multiple times and proliferated to end up in a multifarious complex of sects, each one of them claims to be the true Shīʿa, as the book suggests.

The other important principle is dictated by the need to discuss similar groups together. This way, it is easy to compare the subtle differences among the sects that held mutual doctrines. While, according to the timeline method, one encounters the discussion of sects as they emerged in history, the grouping method shows a succession of one group of sects after another with the possibility of an overlap in time. Al-Nawbakhtī relies on both methods at the same time. Originally, he follows the timeline method; but whenever he reaches a major group of sects (e.g. the Kaysānīyya, the Zaydīyya, or the Ismāʿīlīyya), he follows the timeline of this group until his own era. Then he returns to the major sect, of which the group emerged.

Like his treatment of the rivals of the Shīʿa, al-Nawbakhtī does not attack any of the different groups he disagrees with, as a zealot would. He simply gives accounts of their doctrines and their arguments, sometimes along with the reaction of other groups to such doctrines. His own identity as an *Ithnā ʿAsharī* (Twelver) Shīʿite is discerned throughout the book only by his reverence for the twelve imāms. Whenever he mentions one of them by name, he almost always follows that with the phrase (peace be upon him.) He does not do this with any one else, other than the Prophets and al-ʿAbbās, the uncle of the Prophet, whose name is followed – once – by the phrase "may Allah's mercy be upon him", and the name of Muḥammad b. al-Ḥanafīyya that was followed by the phrase "may Allah, the Exalted, have mercy on his soul."

However, it is not until the end of the book when al-Nawbakhtī explicitly states his position and identity as a Twelver Shīʿite. When he discuses the sect that holds a doctrine about al-Mahdī, which is identical his own, al-Nawbakhtī says: "This doctrine has been the path of establishing the imāmate – it is the doctrine, which the true Shīʿa hold." He calls it the "Imāmīyya". Interestingly, he lists this sect as number twelve among the fourteen sects that emerged after the death of Imam al-Ḥasan al-ʿAskarī (although al-Nawbakhtī mentions fourteen sects, he actually discusses only thirteen of them).

About the Author

Abū Muḥammed, al-Ḥasan b. Mūsā b. al-Ḥasan b. Muḥammad b. al-ʿAbbās b. Ismāʿīl b. Abī Sahl b. Nawbakht, was born in the first half of the third/tenth century. The years of his birth and death are not precisely mentioned anywhere in the history books. However, we can place him quite accurately by assembling the anecdotal accounts that involved him and a number of his contemporaries. Also, al-Najāshī said that he was "the Mutakallim, who surpassed his contemporaries – before the year three hundred [A.H.] and thereafter." This statement places his death very shortly after the turn of the fourth/eleventh century. We also know, from al-Ṭūsī, that Abū Muḥammed was frequently visited by Thābit b. Qurrah (d. 288/900) and Isḥāq b. Ḥunayn (d. 298/910). He also has a book containing his debates with the Muʿtazilite Abū al-Qāsim al-Balkhī (d. 317/929) and his student Abū Jaʿfar [Muḥammad] b. Qubbah; the latter converted to Shīʿism, according to Shaykh al-Ṭūsī.

According to this timeline, al-Nawbakhtī must have been living during the Minor Occultation, which began in 260/864.

Other Works by al-Nawbakhtī

1. *Al-Ārā' wa al-Diyānāt* (unfinished).
2. *Al-Iḥtijāj li 'Umar b. 'Abbās wa Nuṣratu Madhhabihi.*
3. *Ikhtiṣār al-Kawn wa al-Fasād li Arisṭoṭālīs.*
4. *Al-Arzāq wa al-Ājāl wa al-As'ār.*
5. *Al-Istiṭā'ah.*
6. *Al-I'tibār wa al-Tamyīz wa al-Intiṣār.*
7. *Al-Imāmah* (unfinished).
8. *Kitāb al-Insān.*
9. *Al-Tanzīh wa Dhikr Mutashābih al-Qur'ān.*
10. *Al-Tawḥīd wa Ḥudūth al-'Ālam.*
11. *Al-Tawḥīd al-Ṣaghīr.*
12. *Al-Tawḥīd al-Kabīr.*
13. *Al-Tawḍīḥ fī Ḥurūb Amīr al-Mu'minīn (pbuh).*
14. *Al-Jāmi' fī al-Imāmah.*
15. *Fi al-Juz' Alladhī Lā Yatajazza'.*
16. *Jawābatuhu li Ja'far b. Qubbah.*
17. *Ḥujaj Ṭabī'īyya Mustakhraja min Kutubi Arisṭoṭālīs fī al-Raddi 'alā Man Za'ama Anna al-Falaka Ḥayyun Nāṭiq.*
18. *Al-Ḥujaj fī al-Imāmah.*
19. *Kitāb fī Khabar al-Wāḥid wa al-'Amalu bihi.*

20. *Al-Khuṣūṣ wa al-ʻUmūm.*
21. *Al-Radd ʻalā Abī ʻAlī al-Jubbāʼī fī Raddihi ʻalā al-Munajjimīn.*
22. *Al-Radd ʻalā Abī al-Hudhayl al-ʻAllāf fī Anna Naʻīmu Ahl al-Jannati Munqaṭiʻ.*
23. *Al-Radd ʻalā Aṣḥāb al-Tanāsukh.*
24. *Al-Radd ʻalā Aṣḥāb al-Manzilati bayna al-Manzilatayn.*
25. *Al-Radd ʻalā Ahl al-Taʻjīz.*
26. *Al-Radd ʻalā Ahl al-Manṭiq.*
27. *Al-Radd ʻalā Thābit b. Qurrah.*
28. *Al-Radd ʻalā al-Ghulāt.*
29. *Al-Radd ʻalā Firaq al-Shīʻa* [other than the Imāmīyya].
30. *Al-Radd ʻalā al-Mujassima.*
31. *Al-Radd ʻalā Man Akthara al-Munāzala.*
32. *Al-Radd ʻalā Man Qāla bi al-Ruʼyati li al-Bārī ʻAzza wa Jall.*
33. *Al-Radd ʻalā al-Munajjimīn.*
34. *Al-Radd ʻalā al-Wāqifa.*
35. *Al-Radd ʻalā Yaḥyā b. al-Asfaḥ fī al-Imāmah.*
36. *Sharḥ Majālisihi maʻa Abī ʻAbdillāh b. Mumallak.*
37. *Kitāb Firaq al-Shīʻa.*
38. *Majālisuhu maʻa Abī al-Qāsim al-Balkhī.*
39. *Mukhtaṣar al-Kalām fī al-Juzʼ.*
40. *Kitāb fī al-Marāyā wa Jihati al-Ruʼyati fīhā.*

41. *Masā'iluhu li al-Jubbā'ī fī Masā'ila Shattā.*
42. *Al-Naqḍ 'alā Abī al-Hudhayl fī al-Ma'rifa.*
43. *Naqḍ Kitāb Abī 'Īsā [al-Warrāq] fī al-Gharīb al-Mashriqī.*
44. *Al-Naqḍ 'alā Ja'far b. Ḥarb fī al-Imāmah.*
45. *Al-Naqḍ 'alā Ibn al-Rāwandī.*

Shīʿa Sects

Kitāb Firaq al-Shīʿa

Preface

All of the Islamic sects – Shīʿa and others – held different positions about the imāmate, in every era and about every imām – during his life and after his death. This has happened since the death of Muḥammad, peace be upon him, and his family. In this book, we have recorded what has been handed down to us about the sects and their doctrines and differences, in addition to what we recall about the causes of their differences and what we learned from history regarding these matters. We seek support and guidance from Allāh.

The Messenger of Allāh, peace be upon him, and his family, died in the month of Rabīʿ al-Awwal of the tenth year after the *Hijra*.[1] He was then sixty-three years old, of which he, peace be upon him, spent twenty-three years as Prophet. His mother was Āmina bt. Wahab b. ʿAbd Manāf b. Zuhra b. Kilāb b. Murrah b. Kaʿb b. Luʾay b. Ghālib. After his death, Muslims were divided into three sects: one sect was called 'the Shīʿa,' – the Shīʿa of ʿAlī b.

---

[1] *Hijra* literally means the migration. It refers to the migration of the Prophet from Mecca to Medīna in 622 CE. Muslims used this event later to mark the beginning of Islamic calendar.

Abī Ṭālib,[1] peace be upon him, who were divided later to constitute all the sects of the Shīʿa. The second sect claimed the right to the rule and to possess political power (sulṭān); these were the Anṣār[2] (the Supporters [of the Prophet]). They suggested the appointment of Saʿd b. ʿUbāda al-Khazrajī.[3] The third sect tilted towards the appointment of Abū Bakr b. Abī Quḥāfa[4] and based their position on the claim that the Prophet, peace be upon him, and his family, did not specify a particular successor, leaving the matter to the community (*umma*) to choose for itself the preferred person. Some of them cited the story that the Messenger of Allāh, peace be upon him, and his family, ordered him [i.e. Abū Bakr] to lead the

---

[1] ʿAlī b. Abī Ṭālib, the Prophet's cousin and the husband of Fāṭima, the Prophet's daughter. He was the first to believe in his message after the Prophet's wife, Khadījah. He was born ten years before the revelation. He was elected to the caliphate in 35 AH and was assassinated in 40 AH by a Kharijite named Abdul Raḥmān b. Muljam.

[2] When the Prophet migrated to Medīna, its people were called the *Anṣār* or the Supporters of the Prophet. The Meccan migrants were called the *Muhājirūn* (those who migrated to Medīna.

[3] Saʿd b. ʿUbādah al-Khazrajī was the chief of the Khazraj tribe, one of the two major tribes in Medīna. He was the standard bearer for the Anṣār.

[4] Abū Bakr b. Abī Quḥāfa was a companion of the Prophet before and after the revelation. He was also the father of ʿĀʾisha, one of the Prophet's wives. He was elected as the caliph after the death of the Prophet.

prayer, the night he [i.e. the prophet] died. They considered this an evidence of his merit to succeed the prophet, saying, 'the Prophet, peace be upon him, and his family, selected him for our religion and we selected him for our life affairs;' considering his succession binding for everybody. This position led to a dispute between this sect and the Anṣār and ended up at the saqīfa[1] of Banī Sāʿida, with the presence of Abū Bakr, 'Umar,[2] Abū 'Ubayda b. al-Jarrāḥ,[3] and al-Mughīra b. Shuʿba al-Thaqafī.[4] The Anṣār proposed the appointment of Saʿd b. 'Ubāda al-Khazrajī, claiming that they deserved to rule. When their proposal was denied, they suggested power sharing with one ruler from each group (*minnā amīr wa minkum amīr*). The sect of Abū Bakr replied that the Prophet, peace be upon him, said, 'the imāms are from Quraish,' or 'The imāmate is not suitable but to Quraish.' At the end, most of the Anṣār and their supporters yielded to Abū Bakr, except for a small group that remained with Saʿd b. 'Ubāda and

---

[1] The *saqīfa* was the meeting place for Banū Sāʿida, a group of the Khazraj tribe.

[2] 'Umar b. al-Khaṭṭāb was the father of Ḥafṣa, the wife of the Prophet. He was appointed for the caliphate by Abū Bakr, before the latter's death. He was assassinated in 23 AH by a slave named Abū Lu'lu'a.

[3] Abū 'Ubayda 'Āmir b. al-Jarrāḥ was the leader of the army that conquered Syria. He died in the plague of 18 AH.

[4] Al-Mughīra b. Shuʿba became a Muslim in 5 AH. He was appointed governor of Baṣra, then governor of Kūfa, by 'Umar. When 'Uthmān became caliph, he dismissed al-Mughīra from the latter post. He remained away from politics until the reign of Muʿāwiya b. Abī Sufyān, who restored his appointment as the governor of Kūfa. He died in 50 AH.

his family. He did not show loyalty to Abū Bakr until he left for al-Shām (Syria), while on bad terms with Abū Bakr and ʿUmar, and was killed, in Ḥūrān, by the Romans. However, some claimed that he was killed by the *Jinns* and cited the famous poetry which was attributed to the *Jinns*:

'We killed the chief of Khazraj, Saʿd b. ʿUbāda,
We shot two arrows and did not miss his heart.'

This, of course, calls for some thinking, for it is not customary that the *Jinns* shoot arrows at humans and kill them. [Be that as it may,] the vast majority went along with Abū Bakr and remained with him and with ʿUmar – united around them and content with them. Another group seceded from Abū Bakr saying, 'We will not give the alms to him until we are certain of the rightful ruler, the one who was appointed by the Messenger of Allāh, peace be upon him, and him family. Meanwhile we will divide the alms among our own poor and needy people.' Other people renounced Islam, while the Banū Ḥanīfa claimed that Musaylama[1] was a prophet – he already claimed to be prophet during the life of the Messenger of Allāh, peace be upon him, and his family. Abū Bakr sent an army led by Khālid b. al-Walīd b. al-Mughīra al-

[1] Musaylama b. Thumāma al-Ḥanafī is also referred to as Musaylama al-Kadhdhāb (the Liar). He claimed that he was a prophet and wrote some verses imitating the style of the Qur'ān. He was killed in 12 AH, during the battle between his party and the army of Khālid b. al-Walīd (Abū Bakr's general).

Makhzūmī,[1] who fought with them and killed Musaylama, among others, and some of them submitted to Abū Bakr. These were called *Ahl al-Ridda* (people who renounced Islam). They remained united until they became discontent with ʿUthmān b. ʿAffān[2] because of certain things he did.[3] Some of them let him down, while

---

[1] Khālid b. al-Walīd (d. 21 AH) began his military career fighting against the Muslims. Then he converted to Islam and became a general for Abū Bakr and ʿUmar. His biggest achievement was the conquest of Syria.

[2] ʿUthmān b. ʿAffān was the third caliph. He was criticized for favoring his relatives in pay and political appointments despite their lack of merit. When he failed to correct their wrongdoing, a mob of angry people burst into his house and killed him in 35 AH.

[3] ʿUthmān was criticized for several reasons, among them are: (1) he allowed his own uncle, al-Ḥakam b. Abī al-ʿĀṣ, to live again in Medīna, after being banished by the Prophet. Abū Bakr and ʿUmar denied his request to return after the Prophet's death; (2) he favored his own relatives in pay and political positions regardless of their merit. For instance, he appointed al-Walīd b. ʿUqba as the governor of Kūfa, despite al-Walīd's irreligiosity. He then dismissed him because he would appear in public inebriated. He also appointed ʿAbdullah b. Abī Sarh, whose reputation was not better than al-Walīd's, as a governor of Egypt; (3) ʿUthmān was also criticized for causing harm to some eminent companions of the Prophet. Among these were ʿAbdullāh b. Masʿūd, ʿAmmār b. Yāsir, and Abū Dhar; and (4) he was submissive to his cousin, Marwān b. Al-Ḥakam, whose bad counsel and irresponsible

others participated in killing him. Only his close kin and few others remained loyal to him. When he was killed, people gave their allegiance to ʿAlī, peace be upon him, and were called *al-Jamāʿa* (the people of consensus,) then they were divided into three sects: one group remained loyal to ʿAlī b. Abī Ṭālib, peace be upon him.

---

conduct caused the wrath of the masses. See al-Ashʿarī, *Maqālāt al-Islāmiyyīn*, pp. 51-54.

The Divergence After the Assassination of ʿUthmān

Another sect stood aside, along with Saʿd b. Mālik (Saʿd b. Abī Waqqāṣ),[1] ʿAbdullāh b. ʿUmar b. al-Khaṭṭāb,[2] Muḥammad b. Maslama al-Anṣārī,[3] and Usāma b. Zayd b. Ḥāritha al-Kalbī,[4] the servant of the Messenger of Allāh, peace be upon him, and his family. These men stayed away from ʿAlī, peace be upon him, and refused to fight on his side or against him, after having already given

[1] Saʿd b. Abī Waqqāṣ (d. 55 AH) was the conqueror of Iraq. ʿUmar appointed him as the governor of Kūfa, but ʿUthmān dismissed him later.

[2] ʿAbdullāh b. ʿUmar was the second caliph's son. He was one of the transmitters of the Prophet's Ḥadīth, in addition to being a jurist. He contradicted his father in some of his rulings.

[3] One of the companions of the Prophet. He was placed in charge of Medīna during one of the Prophets campaigns. He died in 46 AH.

[4] Usāma b. Zayd (d. 54 AH) was the son of Zayd b. Ḥāritha, the adopted son of the Prophet. Before the Prophet's death, he appointed Usāma as a leader of a campaign and asked his senior companions to fight under his command, despite his very young age. Some companions, including ʿUmar and Abū Bakr, did not go, hence there was a major controversy. See al-Shahrastānī, *al-Milal wa al-Niḥal*, p. 12.

their allegiance to him and accepting his appointment. They were called the Muʿtazila and became the ancestors of the Muʿtazila sects. They said that both fighting against ʿAlī and fighting on his side were religiously not permissible. Some learned people said that al-Aḥnaf b. Qays al-Tamīmī[1] stepped aside later, with his close associates, not out of religious concern, but in order to safeguard his life and property. He said to his people, 'For your own good, stay away from this schism.' Another sect that turned against ʿAlī, peace be upon him, was represented by Ṭalḥa b. ʿAbdillāh,[2] al-Zubayr b. al-ʿAwwām,[3]

---

[1] Al-Aḥnaf b. Qays was the chief of the Tamīm, a major Iraqi tribe. He is often referred to as an exemplary leader whose prudence and wisdom secured the highest positions for him despite his unattractive appearance. He died in 72 AH.

[2] Ṭalḥa b. ʿAbdillāh (d. 36 AH) was among the important companions of the Prophet. He gave his allegiance to Imam ʿAlī and later changed his position. He was killed by one of his allies, Marwān b. al-Ḥakam, during the battle of the Camel, against Imam ʿAlī.

[3] Another prominent companion and a cousin of the Prophet whose attitude towards Imam ʿAlī was mysterious. He was a staunch supporter of the right of ʿAlī to immediately succeed the Prophet, refusing to give allegiance to Abū Bakr. Then he became one of five contestants for the caliphate, running against ʿAlī and four others, but neither him, nor Imam ʿAlī were selected. He emerged again during the caliphate of ʿAlī to dispute his right to rule. After a private conversation between him and ʿAlī, before the battle of the Camel, he became con-

and 'Ā'isha bt. Abī Bakr.[1] They arrived in Baṣra and defeated its governor – appointed by 'Alī, peace be upon him, – and looted the treasury, forcing 'Alī to march to them and defeat them. Ṭalḥa and al-Zubayr were killed. They were called 'the people of the Camel.'[2] Some of them fled and joined Mu'āwiya b. Abī Sufyān[3] and were

---

vinced that his position was wrong and quit the battle before it began, but did not switch sides to join the army of Imam 'Alī. A certain ibn Jarmūz assassinated him on that day.

[1] 'Ā'isha bt. Abī Bakr was the Prophet's wife. She was inciting the Meccans against 'Uthmān, but turned completely to the opposite side and called for the punishment of his killers when she learned that Imam 'Alī was elected to succeed him. She died in 58 AH.

[2] They acquired this name because 'Ā'isha was riding on a camel to observe the fighting. The battle was called "The Battle of the Camel."

[3] Mu'āwiya b. Abī Sufyān (d. 60 AH) was appointed as a governor of Syria by 'Umar b. al-Khaṭṭāb, and was confirmed in his position during the caliphate of 'Uthmān. This allowed him over twenty years to form a semi-independent state, especially during the caliphate of 'Uthmān, who was not interested in keeping his governors in check. He refused to acknowledge the caliphate of Imam 'Alī and the armies of the two had a bloody confrontation at the valley of Ṣiffīn. The fight was stopped and the two agreed for arbitration. Before the resumption of another war, 'Alī was assassinated. Mu'āwiya managed to be acknowledged as a caliph after a truce between him and al-Ḥasan, the oldest son of 'Alī. Mu'āwiya established the first

joined by the Syrians in opposition to ʿAlī. They called for revenging the death of ʿUthmān, accusing ʿAlī, peace be upon him, and his supporters of killing him. They also called for the appointment of Muʿāwiya [as the caliph] and fought against ʿAlī, peace be upon him, in *Ṣiffīn*. Then, one sect left the army of ʿAlī, peace be upon him, and disagreed with him after the arbitration between him and Muʿāwiya. Their motto was, '[There should be] no judgment, but Allāh's.' They considered ʿAlī, peace be upon him, blasphemous and dissociated themselves from him, giving allegiance to Dhu al-Thadya. These were the deserters (*al-Māriqūn*). ʿAlī, peace be upon him, marched to them and fought them in al-Nahrawān, virtually killing all of them, including Dhu al-Thadya. They were called the Harūrīyya – after name of the battle-place (Harūrāʾ). They were also called the Khawārij (*al-Khawārij*) and were the rootstock for all the Khārijite sects.

The Murjiʿa

When ʿAlī, peace be upon him, was assassinated, the people, who were on his side – except for few people among his Shīʿas, who believed in his imāmate after the Prophet, peace be upon him, – joined the sect of Ṭalḥa,

dynasty in Islam, the Umayyads, that began with his twenty-year rule.

al-Zubayr, and ʿĀʾisha. They became a united group under the rule of Muʿāwia b. Abī Sufyān. These were the vast majority and the followers of kings and supporters of the winners – I mean the ones who joined Muʿāwiya – and they were called 'the Murjiʿa' because they supported all of the disputants. They claimed that all Muslims (*Ahl al-Qibla*) are faithful by the virtue of their apparent faith, and they prayed to Allāh to forgive all of them.

The Murjiʿa[1] were divided later into four sects. One sect exaggerated in their doctrines. These were 'the Jahmīyya.' They followed Jahm b. Ṣafwān.[2] These were the Murjiʿa of Khurāsān. Another sect was called 'the Ghaylānīyya.' They followed Ghaylān b. Marwān.[3] These were the Murjiʿa of Syria. A third sect was called 'the

---

[1] The Murjiʿa is a major sect of Islam. The word is derived from "*arjaʿa*," which means "*postponed.*" They acquired this name because they postponed the judgment of grave sinners to the Day of Judgment. See *al-Milal wa al-Niḥal*, p. 137.

[2] Jahm b. Ṣafwān was, according to al-Sharīf al-Murtaḍā, the first to claim that man's actions, including disobedience and blasphemy, are created by Allah; just like his color and other faculties are created by Allah. He also said that it is up to Allah to reward or to punish men for their actions, which He has created (*Rasāʾil* al-Sharīf al-Murtaḍā, vol. II, p. 181). Jahm was captured by Naṣr b. Sayyār, who ordered his killing in 128 AH.

[3] Ghaylān b. Marwān was a man of letters and eloquence. His death came after a debate between him and al-Awzāʿī, the famed jurist. The latter issued a decree to kill Ghaylān. He was killed during the caliphate of Hishām b. ʿAbd al-Malik. See *al-Milal wa al-Niḥal*, p. 140.

Māṣirīyya.' They followed ʿAmr b. Qays al-Māṣir. These were the Murjiʿa of Iraq. Among them was Abū Ḥanīfa and his peers. The fourth sect was called 'the people of doubt' (*al-Shukkāk*) and the Butrīyya[1] – the people of *Ḥadīth*. Among these were Sufyān b. Saʿīd al-Thawri,[2] Sharīk b. ʿAbdillāh,[3] Ibn Abī Laylā,[4] Muḥammad b. Idrīs al-Shāfiʿī,[5] Mālik b. Anas,[1] and their peers – the vast majority – who were also called 'the Ḥashwīyya'.[2]

---

[1] The Butriyya is a Zaydiyya sect. They acquired the name because their chief, Sulaymān b. Jarīr, was called "al-Abtar," because he denied the Prophet's explicit designation of Imam ʿAlī for the caliphate. Some say that Kathīr al-Nawwā' is the one, who was called "al-Abtar." It is also said that they were called "Butriyya" because they do not recite loudly the verse *bismillāh ar-Raḥmān ar-raḥīm* before the second Qur'ānic chapter during the prayer. (*al-Munya wa al-Amal*, p. 91; *al-Farq bayn al-Firaq*, p. 33).

[2] Sufyān al-Thawrī (d. 161 AH) was a prominent transmitter of the Ḥadīth. He lived during the rule of the Umayyads and the ʿAbbāsids. He also made some valuable commentaries on certain parts of the Qur'ān.

[3] Sharīk b. ʿAbdillāh (d. 177 AH) was a contemporary of Sufyān al-Thawrī. He was appointed judge during the caliphate of al-Manṣūr, the second ʿAbbāsid caliph.

[4] Ibn Abī Laylā (d. 148) was a student of Abū Ḥanīfa, the founder of the Hanafi school of jurisprudence.

[5] Al-Shāfiʿī (d. 204 AH) is the founder of the Shāfiʿī school of jurisprudence. He wrote many books in various Islamic sciences, among them are *al-Umm* and *Aḥkām al-Qur'ān*.

[1] Mālik b. Anas (d. 179 AH) is the founder of the Mālikī school of Jurisprudence. He wrote the famed book, *al-Muwaṭṭa'*, which is a large collection of Ḥadīth. He also has authored *Tafsīr Gharīb al-Qur'ān*, a commentary on the peculiar passages of the Qur'ān.

[2] The Ḥashwiyya are those, who accept any Ḥadīth without verifying its authenticity. Their common doctrines are predestination, anthropomorphism, prohibiting the engagement in Kalām debates, and denying the creation of the Qur'ān. See *al-Munya wa al-Amal*, p. 114.

The Divergence About the Imamate

Their elders said the following about the imāmate: 'The Messenger of Allāh, peace be upon him, left this world without appointing any particular person to take his place to unite the people and to discharge the duties of government – such as caring for the people, making treaties, appointing governors, deploying armies, defending the core of Islam, suppressing the opponents, teaching the ignorant, and providing justice for the wronged.' They also assigned this role to anyone who took charge after the Messenger, peace be upon him, and his family.

Then these people disagreed. Some said that people must use their judgment to appoint the imām and that all new problems of life and religion must be dealt with by using opinion (*ijtihād al-ra'y*). Others believed that judgment is erroneous, and that Allāh ordered people to use their reason when choosing the imām. A sect of the Muʿtazila[1] deviated from the belief of their elders when

---

[1] The Muʿtazila is a major sect of Islam. The follwers of this sect built their theology on five doctrines: (1) the unity of God; (2) His justice; (3) the certainty of God's acting upon His threat and promise; (4) the intermediate position of the grave sinner – between being faithful and infidel; and (5) commanding the good and forbidding the evil. They were also known

they said that the Prophet, peace be upon him, specified the character of the imām without specifying his name and lineage. They concocted this doctrine very recently. A sect of the people of *Ḥadīth*, after being crunched by the Imāmīyya[1] argument, resorted to the claim that the Prophet, peace be upon him, and his family, indeed appointed Abū Bakr, by ordering him to lead the prayer. By saying this, they abandoned the doctrine of their elders, who said that Muslims, after the death of the Prophet, peace be upon him, said, 'We accepted for our life an imām, who was accepted for our religion by the Messenger of Allāh, peace be upon him, and his family.'

The proponents of the '*ihmāl*' [i.e. who claimed that the prophet neglected (*ahmala*) to appoint a successor] disagreed about the imāmate of the superior (*fāḍil*) and the inferior (*mafḍūl*). Most of them said that it is permissible for both, if the superior has a problem that hinders his appointment. The rest agreed with the people of *naṣṣ* (explicit designation) about the imāmate being not permissible except for the superior.

They also held different positions regarding Prophet's will (*waṣīyya*). The proponents of '*ihmāl*' (neglect) said: the Messenger of Allāh, peace be upon him, and his family, died without leaving a will or a testament for anyone.

---

for placing high emphasis on reason and rationality in faith and theology.

[1] The Imāmiyya is the main sect of the Shīʿa. Their common doctrines are the Prophet's explicit designation of Imam ʿAlī for the caliphate and the necessity of the imāmate as a political and religious leadership. Their division into many groups, as the author will enumerate, is based on their divergence regarding who the imām is, in any given era.

Others said that his will was ordering people to fear Allāh, the Exalted.

Then they disagreed about the imāmate and its people. The Butrīyya, the followers of al-Ḥasan b. Ṣāliḥ b. Ḥay[1] and his peers, said that ʿAlī, peace be upon him, was the best person after the Messenger of Allāh, peace be upon him, and his family, and the most qualified man for the imāmate. But they said that the appointment of Abū Bakr was not erroneous. However, they abstained from judging ʿUthmān and supported the party of ʿAlī, peace be upon him, and agreed that his opponents deserve Hell fire. They argued that ʿAlī, peace be upon him, yielded to them [i.e. the first two successors] and by doing so, he resembled a man with a legitimate claim against another and decided to drop his claim.

Yet Sulaymān b. Jarīr al-Riqqī[2] and his followers said that ʿAlī, peace be upon him, was the imām and that appointing Abū Bakr and ʿUmar was erroneous, but they cannot be accused of debauchery (*fisq*), because they used their judgment and made a mistake. This sect dissociated itself from ʿUthmān and considered him blasphemous,

[1] Al-Ḥasan b. Ṣāliḥ (d. 168 AH) was a prominent Zaydite. Among his books are *al-Tawḥīd* and *al-Jāmiʿ fi al-Fiqh*. The Ṣāliḥiyya sect of the Zaydiyya are named after him. See *al-Milal wa al-Niḥal*, p. 161.

[2] Sulaymān b. Jarīr al-Riqqī lived during the caliphate of al-Manṣūr, the ʿAbbāsid caliph. The Sulaymāniyya sect of the Zaydiyya was named after him. See *al-Farq bayna al-Firaq*, pp. 32-33.

along with anyone who fought against ʿAlī, peace be upon him.

Ibn al-Tammār[1] and his followers said that ʿAlī, peace be upon him, was the most eligible man for the imāmate and that he was the best person after the Messenger of Allāh, peace be upon him, and his family. But they said that Muslims were not wrong when they appointed Abū Bakr and ʿUmar; they were wrong by forsaking the superior. This group also dissociated themselves from ʿUthmān and considered him and anyone who fought against ʿAlī, peace be upon him, as apostates.

Al-Faḍl al-Raqāshi, Abū Shimr,[2] Ghaylān b. Marwān, Jahm b. Ṣafwān, and their followers among the Murjiʿa said that anyone who has knowledge about the Book and the *Sunna* (tradition of the Prophet) deserves the imāmate. According to them, the imāmate cannot be acquired without unanimous agreement of the Muslim community.

Abū Ḥanīfa[3] and the rest of the Murjiʿa said that the imāmate cannot be outside of the tribe of Quraysh. Anyone from its men, who calls for the Book and the *Sunna* and justice, is the rightful imām. His imāmate as well as fighting on his side become mandatory. They cite the *Ḥadīth* that was attributed to the Prophet, peace be upon him, and his family, 'The imāms are from Quraysh.'

---

[1] The doctrine of Ibn al-Tammār seems identical with that of Sulaymān b. Jarīr.

[2] Abū Shimr was al-Naẓẓām's student. He combined the belief of the Murjiʿa, in postponing judgment on the sinners, and that of the Muʿtazila in disputing predestination.

[3] Abū Ḥanīfa (d. 150 AH) is the founder of the Ḥanafi school of jurisprudence.

All the Khawārij, except for the Najdīyya, said that the imāmate could be assigned to anyone who is knowledgeable about the Book and the *Sunna* and who applies them. They said that the agreement of two men is enough to appoint an imām.

The Najdīyya, however, said that the Muslim community does not need an imām or anyone else; it is simply incumbent, upon us and upon other people, to apply the Book of Allāh, the Exalted.

The Muʿtazila said that the imāmate is deserved by anyone who applies the Book and the *Sunna*. If a man from Quraysh and another man were qualified, we would prefer the former. They also said that the imāmate must be decided based on consensus, free choice, and reason.

Ḍirār b. ʿAmr[1] said that if a man from Quraysh and a non-Arab man were qualified, we must prefer the latter, because he has a smaller tribe. If he disobeys Allāh, it would be easy to remove him from office. This is better for Islam.

Ibrāhīm al-Naẓẓām[2] and his followers said that the imāmate is deserved by any man, who applies the Book and the *Sunna*, for the saying of Allāh, the Exalted, 'The most esteemed among you, before Allāh, is the most pi-

---

[1] Ḍirār b. ʿAmr was a contemporary of Wāṣil b. ʿAṭā'. Bishr b. al-Muʿtamir wrote a book to refute him, titled *ar-Rad 'ala Ḍirār*. Al-Khayyāṭ attributed a book to Ḍirār titled *al-Taḥrīsh* which – he said – contained descriptions of the doctrines of each sect. (See *al-Intiṣār*, pp. 136-37)

[2] Ibrāhīm al-Naẓẓām (d. 221 AH) was a prominent Muʿtazilite scholar. He was the nephew of Abū al-Hudhayl al-ʿAllāf.

ous' (Qur'ān, 49:13). They claimed that people are not obligated to appoint an imām if they obey Allāh and purify their conduct and intention. That is not possible without knowing the imām, who must be obeyed; since Allāh, the Exalted, would not mandate that they recognize an imām without providing them with the knowledge of recognizing him. Otherwise, He would be mandating that which is impossible.

They said that Muslims were correct in appointing Abū Bakr, because he was the most suitable among them, according to analogy and history. As to analogy, we know that a man does not submit to another and follow his orders unless three conditions obtain. Either the latter has a large clan to help him control others, or he has money that makes people submit to him, or he has a religious status that distinguishes him among others. We know that Abū Bakr was a man with the smallest clan and the least assets; therefore it is certain that he was preferred because of his religious status. And the historical evidence is that he acquired the consensus of people and their acceptance of his imāmate. The Prophet, peace be upon him, and his family, said, 'Allāh, the Exalted, would not allow my people to agree on error.' If the consensus of the people about him was an error, then the prayer and all other religious duties would be invalid and the Qur'ān – which is the only source of our religion after the death of the Prophet peace be upon him – would be obsolete. This is the Muʿtazila argument, which is also the argument of all of the Murjiʿa sects.

ʿAmr b. ʿUbayd,[1] Ḍirār b. ʿAmr, and Wāṣil b. ʿAṭā'[2] were the rootstock of the Muʿtazila. ʿAmr b. ʿUbayd and his followers said that ʿAlī, peace be upon him, was more deserving [of the imāmate] than the others. But Ḍirār said, 'I do not know which one was more guided, ʿAlī or Ṭalḥa and az-Zubayr.' Wāṣil b. ʿAṭā' said that ʿAlī and his opponents were like two disputants, whose veracity is not ascertained so that we do not know who is lying and who is telling the truth. These three scholars agreed on loyalty to all of the disputants – as a group – but believed that one of them must be misguided and will undoubtedly go to Hell. They also said that, if ʿAlī, Ṭalḥa, and az-Zubayr gave testimony, after their fight, about a matter of a Dirham's worth, their testimony would not be considered. Yet, if ʿAlī were a witness and he were supported by another man from the community, his testimony would be accepted; and the same goes for Ṭalḥa and az-Zubayr. They considered them [i.e. ʿAlī, Ṭalḥa, and az-Zubayr] faithful, *as a group*, and on the basis of their faithful past, but they did not consider any one of them faithful or a qualified witness (as an individual).

---

[1] ʿAmr b. ʿUbayd (d. 144 AH) was one of the founders of the Muʿtazila sect.

[2] Wāṣil b. ʿAṭā' (d. 181 AH) was the founder of the Muʿtazila sect. He was a student of al-Ḥasan al-Baṣrī, the famed jurist and transmitter of Ḥadīth and the two had a disagreement about the position of the grave sinner. This disagreement ended in permanent divergence between Wāṣil and his teacher.

The Butrīyya, or the People of *Ḥadīth,* al-Ḥasan b. Ṣāliḥ b. Ḥay,[1] Kathīr al-Nawwā',[2] Sālim b. Abī Ḥafṣah,[3] al-Ḥakam b. 'Utayba,[4] Salama b. Kuhayl,[5] Abū al-Miqdām Thābit al-Ḥaddād,[6] and their followers, called for loyalty to 'Alī, peace be upon him, then they mixed it with the loyalty to Abū Bakr and 'Umar. They agreed that 'Alī was the best and the superior among his community. Nevertheless, they accept the judgment of Abū Bakr and 'Umar and allow the wiping of shoes (in the ablution) and permit drinking intoxicating wine and eating catfish.

---

[1] Al-Ḥasan b. Ṣāliḥ b. Ḥay (d. 168 AH) was a prominent Zaydiyya chief. He went into hiding after the death of Zayd b. 'Alī, and remained a fugitive until he died.

[2] Kathīr al-Nawwā' was a contemporary of al-Ḥasan b. Ṣāliḥ b. Ḥay. He was named al-Nawwā' because of his trade, selling date stones (*nawā*).

[3] Abū Yūnus Sālim b. Abī Ḥafṣah (d. 137 AH) was a Persian client (*mawlā*) of the Kūfan 'Ijl tribe.

[4] Al-Ḥakam b. 'Utayba (d. 114 AH) was a Kūfan from the Kinda tribe.

[5] Salama b. Kuhayl (d. 121 AH) was a Kūfan whose transmission of Ḥadīth was accepted by Sufyān al-Thawrī, the famed scholar of Ḥadīth.

[6] Abū al-Miqdām was a Persian client of the 'Ijl tribe.

The Divergence About the Wars of Imām ʿAlī

Muslims disagreed also about the wars of ʿAlī, peace be upon him, against those who fought him:

The Shīʿa, the Zaydīyya,[1] and, from the Muʿtazila, Ibrāhīm b. Sayyār al-Naẓẓām and Bishr b. al-Muʿtamir,[2] and from the Murjiʿa, Abū Ḥanīfa, Abū Yūsuf, and Bishr al-Miryasi[3] said that ʿAlī, peace be upon him, was right in his war against Ṭalḥa and az-Zubayr and the others. They said that of all the opponents, who fought ʿAlī, peace be upon him, were wrong and it was incumbent upon people to fight them and to side with ʿAlī, peace be upon him.

---

[1] Al-Nawbakhtī refers to the Shīʿa and the Zaydiyya here as two different sects. However, in the course of the book, he lists the Zaydiyya as one of the Shīʿa sect. This means that he has two meanings for the word "Shīʿa": the broad meaning, which includes the Zaydiyya; and another narrower meaning that refers to the Imāmiyya.

[2] Abū Sahl Bishr b. al-Muʿtamir (d. 210 AH) was a prominent Muʿtazilite. He founded the Muʿtazila school of Baghdād. He composed a poem of forty thousand verses to rebut the doctrines of his opponents. See *al-Farq bayn al-Firaq*, p. 156.

[3] Bishr b. Ghiyāth al-Miryasī (d. 218 AH) was the head of the Miryasiyya sect. He was a Persian client.

Their evidence was the saying of Allāh, the Exalted, 'Fight the sect that transgresses until it submits to the command of Allāh.' (Qur'ān, 49:9) Therefore, it was incumbent to fight them because they asked that which was not theirs, such as seeking revenge for the killing of ʿUthmān, and by doing so, they transgressed against [ʿAlī]. Another evidence was the statement attributed to ʿAlī, peace be upon him, 'I was ordered to fight the recanters (*an-Nākithīn*), the transgressors (*al-Qāṣiṭīn*) and the deserters (*al-Māriqīn*).' He indeed fought them and, therefore, it was obligatory [for the people] to fight them.

Bakr, the nephew of ʿAbdul-Wāḥid,[1] and his followers said that ʿAlī, Ṭalḥa, and az-Zubayr were polytheists and hypocrites. But they will, nevertheless, go to Paradise because the Messenger of Allāh, peace be upon him, said, 'Allāh, the Exalted, looked at the fighters of Badr[2] and told them: "Do as you please, for I have forgiven you."'

The rest of the Muʿtazila, Ḍirār b. ʿAmr, Maʿmar[3] and Abū al-Hudhayl al-ʿAllāf,[1] as well as the rest of the

---

[1] Bakr b. Ziyād al-Bāhilī was the nephew of Abdul-Wāḥid b. Zayd. He was the head of the Bakriyya sect. He adopted the doctrines of the Muʿtazilite al-Naẓẓām, in addition to opinions of his own, such as the prohibition of eating onion and garlic. See *al-Farq bayn al-Firaq*, pp. 212-13.

[2] Badr was the site of the first battle between the Muslims and the Meccan pagans, known as the Battle of Badr (2 AH). Despite being outnumbered, the Muslims emerged victorious at the end of this battle.

[3] Abū ʿAmr Maʿmar b. ʿAbbād al-Sulamī (d. 220 AH) claimed that Allah did not create the incidents that occur to the bodies. See *al-Farq bayna al-Firaq*, p. 151-154.

Murjiʿa said: "We know that one sect was right and the other was wrong. Therefore, we are loyal to every one of them – as an individual – but we are not loyal to all of them – as a group. Their evidence is that every one of these disputants was unanimously considered to be just and could not be considered unjust without unanimity.

The Ḥashwīyya and Abū Bakr al-Aṣamm[2] said that ʿAlī, Ṭalḥa, and az-Zubayr were wrong in their fighting, and the people who abstained from the war were right. While they are against the war, these people are loyal to all the disputants. They left their dispute for the judgment of Allāh.

Muslims also disagreed about the arbitration:

The Khawārij said that both of the arbiters were blasphemous and ʿAlī too was blasphemous for asking them to arbitrate. Their evidence was the statements of Allāh, the Exalted, "Those, who do not judge according to

---

[1] Abū al-Hudhayl al-ʿAllāf (d. 235) was named after the neighborhood where he lived, the quarter of *al-ʿAllāfīn* (sellers of hay). He was the first acknowledged Muʿtazilite chief. Ibn al-Murtaḍā said that al-ʿAllāf wrote sixty books defending his doctrines. See *al-Munya wa al-Amal*, p. 149.

[2] Abū Bakr ʿAbd al-Raḥmān b. Kaysān al-Aṣamm was a leading Muʿtazilite. Ibn al-Murtaḍā raved about his prominence, saying: "He was one of the most eloquent, the most knowledgeable, and the most pious – except for his criticism of some actions of ʿAlī [b. Abī Ṭālib], peace be upon him." See *al-Munya wa al-Amal*, p. 156.

Allāh's revelation are the blasphemous;"[1] (Qurʾān, 5:44) and "Those, who do not judge according to Allāh's revelation are the oppressors;" (Qurʾān, 5:45) and "Those, who do not judge according to Allāh's revelation are the debauchers." (Qurʾān, 5:47) They also cited His saying, "Fight the sect that transgresses until it submits to the command of Allāh." (Qurʾān, 49:9) They said that his halting of the war was blasphemy. The Shīʿa, the Murjiʿa, Ibrāhīm al-Naẓẓām, and Bishr b. al-Muʿtamir said that ʿAlī, peace be upon him, was right when he agreed to ar-

[1] Al-Nawbakhtī wrote this verse and merged the other two with it, because the three verses are identical except for the last word in each verse. It reads as follows: "Those, who do not judge according to Allah's revelation are the blasphemous; the oppressors; the debauchers." Although it is customary to write semi-identical Qurʾānic verses in this way for the sake of brevity, it can be confusing for certain readers. Indeed, Dr. ʿAbd al-Munʿim al-Ḥifni believed that both al-Nawbakhtī and al-Qummī cited the verse erroneously by adding two words to it. He did not see three verses, but one that was misquoted. See al-Ḥifni (ed.), *Kitāb Firaq al-Shīʿa*, footnote 3, p. 26.

bitration[1] – seeing that his followers were determined to hold the arbitration and unwilling to fight – and that he agreed in order to unite the Muslims. He ordered the two arbiters to judge according to the Book of Allāh, the Exalted, but they strayed. Therefore, they were wrong and he was right. Their evidence was that the Messenger of Allāh, peace be upon him, made a truce with the people of Mecca and returned Abū Jandal Suhayl b. ʿAmr,[2] in chains, to the pagans. He also requested the arbitration of

[1] The battle of *Ṣiffīn* was about to end in favor of Imām ʿAlī, but the Army of Muʿāwiya was ordered to raise copies of the Qur'ān on the lances and call for an arbitration between the two parties according to the Qur'ān. Imām ʿAlī ordered his soldiers to fight on, but they disobeyed and forced him to accept the offer. The party of Muʿāwiya presented ʿAmr b. al-ʿĀṣ to represent their side and the party of ʿAlī – against his advice – selected Abū Mūsā al-Ashʿarī, who was not a match for the conniving ʿAmr. Abū Mūsā was manipulated and talked into removing ʿAlī from the caliphate in a process that had nothing to do with the arbitration mandate, which was to judge according to the Qurʿān. Consequently, Muʿāwiya bought time to regroup and also found a basis for claiming the caliphate.

[2] Suhayl b. ʿAmr (d. 18 AH) was one of the chiefs in Quraysh. The Muslims captured him during the Battle of Badr. He became a Muslim after the Muslims controlled Mecca.

Saʿd b. Muʿādh[1] between him and the Jews of Banu Qurayẓah and [Banu] al-Naḍīr.

Abū Bakr al-Aṣamm said that the campaign [of ʿAlī] was wrong from the beginning, and the arbitration was wrong too; and that Abū Mūsā al-Ashʿarī[2] was right in removing him, so that the people would unite with an imām.

The rest of the Muʿtazila said that every person who makes a judgment, is right; and that ʿAlī, peace be upon him, made a judgment and he is not to be questioned in his claim, for he was right.

The Ḥashwīyya said, "We do not say anything about these matters. We leave their judgment to Allāh, the Exalted, Who is the best to distinguish between right and error. Meanwhile, we are loyal to all of them on the basis of their first [faithful] status."

All of these types and sects, from the Murjiʿa to the Khawārij, are disagreeing with one another, making many sects – too many to be mentioned here. They accuse each other of being sinful regarding [their beliefs] about the imāmate, jurisprudence, religious decrees, and the doctrine of God's unity, among other religious sciences. They refute one another and accuse one another of being blasphemous. Yet, the most notable thing about them is their

---

[1] Saʿd b. Muʿādh was the chief of al-Aws, one of the two major tribes in Medīna. He was selected by the two Jewish tribes to be the arbiter between them and the Prophet.

[2] He was appointed the governor of Yemen, by the Prophet; then the governor of Baṣra, by ʿUmar; then the governor of Kūfa, by ʿUthmān. He was responsible for the fiasco of the arbitration between Muʿāwiya and Imām ʿAlī, which led him to quit public life.

description of themselves as "the *Jamāʿa*" (united community). They probably refer to their *unity* in giving loyalty to whoever seizes the power over them, whether he is honest or a debauchee. Therefore, their name, "the *Jamāʿa*," does not refer to unity of religion. Indeed, their true condition is that of unequivocal divergence.

Thus, all sects may be classified under four sects: the Shīʿa, the Muʿtazila, the Murjiʿa, and the Khawārij.

The Shīʿa of ʿAlī

The first sect is the Shīʿa. They are the party of ʿAlī b. Abī Ṭālib, peace be upon him, who are also called *Shīʿatu ʿAlī*," peace be upon him, during the life of the Prophet, peace be upon him, and his family, as well as after his life. They were known for supporting him [i.e. ʿAlī] and believing in his imāmate.

Among these were al-Miqdād b. al-Aswad,[1] Salmān al-Fārisī,[2] Abū Dhar Jundub b. Junāda al-Ghafārī,[1] ʿAmmār

---

[1] Al-Miqdād b. al-Aswad (d. 33 AH) was one of the first seven people to declare their conversion to Islam.

[2] Abū ʿAbdillāh Salmān al-Fārisi (d. 36 AH) was highly esteemed by the Prophet, who said, "Salmān is one of us, the family of the Prophet (*ahl al-Bayt*)." His suggestion to dig a moat in the warpath of the enemy helped save the Muslim army from an imminent defeat in the year 5 AH. He was ap-

b. Yāsir,[2] and whoever agreed with ʿAlī, peace be upon him. They were the first [Muslims] to be called with this name, although the word "*Shīʿa*" is an old term since the *Shīʿa* of Ibrāhīm (Abraham), the *Shīʿa* of Mūsā (Moses), the *Shīʿa* of ʿĪsā (Jesus), and the other prophets, peace be upon them. When the Prophet died, peace be upon him, and his family, the Shīʿa split into three sects: one said that ʿAlī, peace be upon him, is an imām, whose commands were binding for all people, after the Messenger of Allāh, peace be upon him, and his family. They must listen to him and take their instructions from him, and anyone else would not qualify. The Prophet, peace be upon him, and his family, trusted him with all the knowledge, which is needed by the people for religious matters, like the permissible acts and the prohibited and every benefit and harm in religious and temporal matters. The prophet trusted him with all forms of knowledge, small or great and made sure that he memorized them. That is why he deserved the imāmate and the leading position that was held by the Prophet, peace be upon him, and his

---

pointed by Imām ʿAlī to govern Medāʾin where he later died. The Shīʿa still visit his shrine to pay him their respect.

[1] Abū Dhar (d. 31 AH) was the fifth person to convert to Islam. He participated in all battles on the Prophet's side. He was known for his piety and ascetic life. His opposition to the wasteful behavior during the caliphate of ʿUthmān forced the latter to exile Abū Dhar from Medīna.

[2] ʿAmmār b. Yāsir (d. 37 AH) was one of the first Muslims. He supported Imām ʿAlī in his wars and was killed during the battle of *Ṣiffīn*. He was treated harshly during the caliphate of ʿUthmān for the same reasons that sent Abū Dhar to exile.

family, for his infallibility (*ʿiṣma*), purity (*ṭahāra*), seniority (*sābiqa*), knowledge, generosity, asceticism (*zuhd*), and justice in dealing with his subjects. The Prophet, peace be upon him, and his family, appointed him and referred to him by name and lineage and left the community under his imāmate, making him the chief and the Commander of the Faithful. He gave him more authority in people's affairs than their own authority. This happened on many occasions, especially at *Ghadīr Khum*.[1] He also told them that the rank of [ʿAlī] is similar to the rank of Aaron in relation to Moses, peace be upon them, though there is no prophet after [Muḥammad]. This was the evidence for his imāmate, for there is no sense here other than the Prophethood and the imāmate. The Prophet also considered him his own counterpart, in that he has more authority in people's affairs than their own authority. During the life of the Prophet, peace be upon him, and his family, he told the Bani Wulayʿa, "give up or I will send to you a man like myself." The position of the Prophet, peace be upon him, and his family, cannot be given to any man, who is not like him, and the imāmate is one of the most significant affairs after the Prophethood. They

[1] *Ghadīr Khum* is a well between Mecca and Medīna. When the Prophet returned from his last pilgrimage, he stopped all his companions at this place and told them, in a long speech, "He who has me as a master must now also have ʿAlī as a master (*man kuntu mawlāhu ahādhā ʿAlīyyun mawlāh*). There is a dispute between the Shīʿa and their Sunni opponents on whether this statement constitutes explicit appointment for the caliphate.

said that [ʿAlī] must be succeeded by a man from his progeny – from the children of Fāṭima, daughter of Muḥammad, peace be upon them. He must be immune from sins, free of imperfections, pious, pure, trustworthy, free of ailments concerning his religion and lineage; and immune from deliberate and unintentional errors. He must also be appointed – by name - by the imām before him. Anyone who becomes his ally will survive and anyone who becomes his foe will have blasphemed and will perish; and anyone who supports another [imām] will be misguided and be considered a polytheist. The imāmate will run in his posterity as long as Allāh's commands and prohibitions remain. This sect remained under his imāmate until ʿAlī, peace be upon him, was assassinated in the month of Ramaḍān. ʿAbd al-Raḥmān b. Muljam,[1]

---

[1] After their catastrophic defeat in the Battle of *Nehrawān*, three Kharijite men (ʿAbd al-Raḥmān b. Muljam, Bark b. ʿAbdullāh, and ʿAmr b. Bakr) conspired to kill ʿAlī, Muʿāwiya, and ʿAmr b. al-ʿĀṣ (Muʿāwiya's governor of Egypt). The plot was to be carried out on the same day, at the dawn prayer. ʿAmr b. al-ʿĀṣ was ill on that day. He ordered his deputy; a man named Khārija, to substitute for him in leading the prayer. The assassin, not acquainted with his mark, took the deputy's life instead. Bark was so nervous that he struck Muʿāwiya on the buttocks. He survived and lived twenty years thereafter. The fate of ʿAlī was the most tragic. During his prayer, he was struck on his head with a sword that was left in strong poison for forty days. It was reported that he knew about the plot. When he was advised to kill or banish the assassin-to-be, he replied: "Punishment cannot precede the crime."

may Allāh curse him, struck him on the nineteenth night of the month, and he died on Sunday, the twenty-first night of Ramaḍān, the year forty after the Hijrah. He was sixty-three years old; the duration of his imāmate was thirty years and the duration of his caliphate was four years and nine months. His mother was Fāṭima bt. Asad b. Hāshim b. ʿAbd Manāf, may Allāh be pleased with them. He was the first Hāshimite, whose mother and father were Hāshimites.

The Shīʿa Divergence After the Assassination of ʿAlī

The Zaydīyya[1]

Another sect said that ʿAlī was the closest of people to themselves, after the Messenger of Allāh, peace be upon him, and his family, because of his merits, seniority, and knowledge. They said that he was the best of all people, after [the Prophet], the most courageous, the most generous, the most pious, and the greatest ascetic. Yet, they accepted the imāmate of Abū Bakr and ʿUmar and considered them fit for the position, saying that ʿAlī, peace be upon him, relinquished the position to them and he agreed to their rule and voluntarily gave them his allegiance, giving up his rights. Therefore, they said, "We consent to whom he consented to, for it is unlawful for us to do otherwise." They said that the allegiance to Abū

---

[1] The Zaydiyya sects did not emerge immediately after the assassination of Imām ʿAlī. They must be discussed among the sects that emerged after the death of ʿAlī b. al-Ḥusayn b. ʿAlī b. Abī Ṭālib, the father of Zayd. The discussion of these sects in this place seems a digression on al-Nawbakhtī's part, as he referred to the founders of their doctrines. He will revisit the Zaydiyya sects later in the book.

Bakr became legitimate because of the consent of ʿAlī, without which Abū Bakr would be erroneous and misguided, and he would perish. These were the founders of the Butrīyya.

From this sect, another sect emerged, saying that ʿAlī, peace be upon him, was the best of all people because of his kin to the Messenger of Allāh, peace be upon him, and his family, and his seniority and knowledge. But it was permissible for the people to appoint another man to rule over them, if the chosen man was qualified for the position, whether he liked it or not. They said that the appointment of the man they chose is rightful and it goes along with the acts of obedience of Allāh, the Exalted, and listening to this man was mandated by Allāh, the Exalted. Therefore, whoever would disagree with him from Quraysh and Banū Hāshim – be it ʿAlī or another man – would be misguided and blasphemous.

Another sect from among these is called the Jārūdīyya. They preferred ʿAlī, peace be upon him, and said that his role could not be given to anyone else. They claimed that anyone, who pushed ʿAlī away from that position, was blasphemous; and that the community was blasphemous and misguided when it abstained from giving the allegiance to him. This sect designated the imāmate, after him for his sons, al-Ḥasan, and then to al-Ḥusayn, peace be upon them. After that, it would be decided by consultation (*shūrā*) among their sons; whoever sought to rule would be deserving the imāmate, if he qualifies. The two (latter) sects were the ones claiming to follow Zayd b. ʿAlī

b. al-Ḥusayn[1] and Zayd b. al-Ḥasan b. ʿAlī b. Abī Ṭālib. The Zaydīyya sects emerged and proliferated from them.

The Saba'īyya

When ʿAlī, peace be upon him, was assassinated, the sect that believed that his imāmate was mandated by Allāh, the Exalted, and his Messenger, peace be upon him, was split into three sects. One sect said that ʿAlī was not killed and that he did not die. They said that he would not die until he had driven the Arabs with his cane and filled the earth with justice and fairness, after it has been filled with oppression and injustice. This was the first sect in Islam that believed in *waqf* (considering ʿAlī the hidden imām), after the Prophet, peace be upon him, and his family. They were also the first extremists (*Ghulāt*). They were called "the Saba'īyya," the followers

---

[1] Zayd b. ʿAlī b. al-Ḥusayn revolted in Kūfa against the Umayyad caliph, Hishām b. ʿAbd al-Malik. He was betrayed by the majority of his followers, but continued to fight until he was killed. The governor of Kūfa, Yūsuf al-Thaqafī found his grave. He gave orders to exhume his body and crucify it.

of ʿAbdullāh b. Sabaʾ,[1] who publicly criticized Abū Bakr, ʿUmar, ʿUthmān, and the Companions. He said that ʿAlī, peace be upon him, ordered him to do that. When ʿAlī asked him about this claim, he admitted saying it, therefore ʿAlī condemned him to death. People said to him, "O Commander of the Faithful! Are you going to kill a man for encouraging people to love you and be loyal to you and dissociate themselves from your enemies?" Then, he expelled him to the city of al-Madāʾin. Some scholars, who were close to ʿAlī, peace be upon him, said that ʿAbdullāh b. Sabaʾ was a Jew before he converted to Islam. He became loyal to ʿAlī, peace be upon him. Before becoming a Muslim, he used to say that Yūshaʿ b. Nūn[2] was the rightful successor after Mūsā, peace be upon him; when he converted to Islam, he said the same

---

[1] There is a controversy regarding the identity of ʿAbdullāh b. Sabaʾ. Al-Nawbakhtī and Saʿd b. ʿAbdillāh al-Qummī were the only Shīʿite scholars who mentioned him. Among the majority of Sunni scholars, it is the conventional wisdom that ʿAbdullāh b. Sabaʾ is the founder of Shīʿism, and therefore, it is a heretic movement that was primarily concocted to destroy Islam. Yet, among the Sunni scholars, some people believe that it is a "fictitious personality." Tāha Ḥusayn, the famed Egyptian scholar, expressed his concern that no historians mentioned this person in their accounts about the Battle of *Ṣiffin*. (*al-Fitna al-Kubrā: ʿAlī wa Banūh*, p. 99.) For more on this subject, see Dr. ʿAlī al-Wardi, *Wuʿʿẓ as-Salāṭīn*, pp. 95-115.

[2] He was a servant of Moses and became later a leader of the Banū Isrāʾīl, succeeding Moses.

thing about ʿAlī, peace be upon him. He was the first to declare that the imāmate of ʿAlī was mandatory. He also publicly denounced his enemies and his opponents. Hence, the opponents of the Shīʿa attributed the origin of *Rafḍ* to Judaism. When he heard that ʿAlī had died, he told the reporter, "You are lying! Even if you bring his brain in seventy parts and have seventy witnesses to support you, we would still know that he did not die. He will not die before he rules the entire world."

The ʿAbbāsīyya

Another sect believed in the imāmate of Muḥammad b. al-Ḥanafīyya,[1] because he was the standard-bearer for his father during the war in Baṣra, unlike his two brothers. This sect was called "the ʿAbbāsīyya," because their chief, al-Mukhtār b. ʿUbayda al-Thaqafī,[2] was called

[1] Muḥammad b. al-Ḥanafiyya (d. 81 AH) was the brother of al-Ḥasan and al-Ḥusayn. He was named after his mother to indicate that he was not the son of Fāṭima – daughter of the Prophet.

[2] Al-Mukhtār b. ʿUbayda al-Thaqafī (d. 67 AH) revolted in Kūfa and brought to justice all the killers of al-Ḥusayn b. ʿAlī. The Shīʿa deny the allegations of his being from the ʿAbbāsīyya. There is a tomb for him inside the shrine of Muslim b. ʿAqīl, in Kūfa that is visited until these days by devout Shīʿites.

"*Kaysān*." He brought to justice the killers of al-Ḥusayn b. ʿAlī, peace be upon him, and his companions. He claimed that Muḥammad b. al-Ḥanafīyya ordered him to do that, and that Muḥammad b. al-Ḥanafīyya was the imām after his father. Al-Mukhtār was called "*Kaysān*" because his chief of police, Abū ʿAmrah, was named *Kaysān*. He was more zealous than al-Mukhtār in his speech, deeds, and killings. He held that Muḥammad b. al-Ḥanafīyya was the heir of ʿAlī b. Abī Ṭālib and that he was the imām, and that al-Mukhtār was his representative and governor. He also considered a blasphemer everyone who ruled before ʿAlī, in addition to those who fought him in *Ṣiffīn* and in the Battle of the Camel. He claimed that Gabriel, peace be upon him, was visiting al-Mukhtār, bringing revelation from Allāh, the Exalted, but [al-Mukhtār] does not see him. It was also said that [al-Mukhtār was called *Kaysān* after the name of a servant of ʿAlī, peace be upon him, who exhorted him to revenge for the murder of al-Ḥusayn b. ʿAlī, peace be upon him, and led him to the killers. He was his confidant and partner in his plot and overseer.

Those Who Believed in the Imamate of al-Ḥasan

Another sect continued to believe in the imāmate of al-Ḥasan b. ʿAlī[1] after his father, except for a small circle, who disputed his imāmate and opposed him after he made a truce with Muʿāwiya and accepted his money. This small circle adopted the opinion of the rest of the community, while his partisans continued to believe in his imāmate until he was killed. When he quit the fight against Muʿāwiya and went to *Sābāṭ*, a man named al-Jarrāḥ b. Sinān jumped on him and grabbed the reigns of his mount saying, "God is great! You have become blasphemous, just like your father." He stabbed him in his thigh cutting it to the bone. al-Ḥasan fell down, hugging al-Jarrāḥ until the people gathered and killed him. Al-Ḥasan was carried to al-Madāʾin and remained in the care of Saʿd b. Masʿūd al-Thaqafī until he recovered. He moved thereafter to Medīna and remained there carrying his wound and suppressing his anger and enduring the bitterness of abuse that came from his own party until he died, peace be upon him, at the end of Safar of the forty-seventh year (AH). His age was forty-five years and six months. Some say that he was born [on the fifteenth] of

[1] Al-Ḥasan b. ʿAlī (d. 47 AH) was the oldest son of ʿAlī and Fāṭima. He was elected for the caliphate after his father, but decided to accept the offer of Muʿāwiya to have a truce, on the condition of his being the caliph after Muʿāwiya. His death before Muʿāwiya allowed the latter to appoint his own son, Yazīd to succeed him.

Ramaḍān in the third year (AH). The duration of his imāmate was six years and five months. His mother is Fāṭima, the daughter of the Messenger of Allāh, peace be upon them, and the daughter of Khadījah b. Khuwaylid b. Asad b. ʿAbd al-ʿUzzā b. Quṣay b. Kilāb.

Those Who Believed in the Imamate of al-Ḥusayn

This sect, which believed in the imāmate of al-Ḥasan b. ʿAlī after his father, believed in the imāmate of his brother, al-Ḥusayn[1], peace be upon them. It continued on

---

[1] Al-Ḥusayn b. ʿAlī (d. 61 AH) was the second son of ʿAlī and Fāṭima. He was martyred in Karbalāʾ, after he refused to acknowledge the appointment of Yazīd for the caliphate. The tragedy of Karbalāʾ legitimized the concept of revolution against oppressive rulers, who profess Islam and act contrary to its principles. However, many non-Shīʿite scholars advocate the doctrine that prohibits revolution, even against oppressive rulers. See Ibn Khaldūn, *Muqaddima*, p. 217.

this belief until he was killed during the days of Yazīd,[1] may Allāh curse him. The man responsible for killing him was ʿUbaydullāh b. Ziyād,[2] said to be the son of Abū Sufyān.[3] The mother ʿUbaydullāh was Marjāna. He was Yazīd's governor in Kūfa and Baṣra. He sent the armies to the desert to meet al-Ḥusayn and they escorted him to

---

[1] Yazīd b. Muʿāwiya (d. 64 AH) was appointed for the caliphate by his father. Unlike his father, who pretended to adhere to Islam, Yazīd was the first ruler to break all the rules. During his four years in office, al-Ḥusayn b. ʿAlī was killed, Medīna was destroyed and thousands of innocent people were slaughtered, and Mecca was attacked. His troops killed people at the Kaʿba, inside the Mecca Mosque.

[2] ʿUbaydullāh b. Ziyād (d. 67 AH) was Yazīd's governor on Kūfa. He was responsible for the murder of al-Ḥusayn b. ʿAlī in Kūfa. He was killed by al-Mukhtār's officer, Ibrāhīm b. al-Ashtar.

[3] Ziyād's mother was married to an ordinary man, but she claimed that she had an affair with Abū Sufyān – the father of Muʿāwiya – and that he is the father of Ziyād. Abū Sufyān did not acknowledge her claim. Muʿāwiya acknowledged Ziyād as his brother to make him desert ʿAlī b. Abī Ṭālib and join him. By doing so, Muʿāwiya ignored the Islamic rule that says: "The child belongs to the husband." Ziyād was then called "Ziyād b. Abīh" (Ziyād, son of his father) to indicate that the identity of his father was not established.

Karbalāʾ.[1] Then ʿUbaydullāh, may Allāh curse him, sent ʿUmar b. Saʿd b. Abī Waqqāṣ[2] to lead the fight. ʿUmar b. Saʿd, may Allāh curse him, killed al-Ḥusayn. He, peace be upon him, was killed in Karbalāʾ on Monday, the tenth day of Muharram in the year sixty-one (AH). His age was fifty-six years and five months. His mother is Fāṭima, the daughter of the Messenger of Allāh, peace be upon them. When al-Ḥusayn was killed, some of his companions became perplexed. They said, "the behavior of al-Ḥasan was the opposite of the behavior of al-Ḥusayn. If the truce of al-Ḥasan and Muʿāwiya and his abdication was right and obligatory (*wājib*), since he was not prepared for war despite the big number of his supporters; then al-Ḥusayn's fight against Yazīd, despite the excessive difference between his supporters and their enemy, which ended in their death, must be erroneous. al-Ḥusayn, they said, would have better excuses, if he were to make a truce, than his brother. However, if al-Ḥusayn's *jihād* against Yazīd b. Muʿāwiya, and his death and the death of his sons and companions, were right and obligatory, then al-Ḥasan's retreat and quitting of the *jihād* against Muʿāwiya, despite [al-Ḥasan's] large army, was erroneous." They had doubts about the imāmate of both brothers and adopted the belief of the general community. The

---

[1] Karbalāʾ is a city in Iraq, where al-Ḥusayn was killed. It is now a holy site for the Shīʿites, who visit it from all around the world.

[2] ʿUmar b. Saʿd (d. 66 AH) was the officer who led the army to fight al-Ḥusayn. Al-Mukhtār killed him, along with the other men responsible for the tragedy of Karbalāʾ.

rest of al-Ḥusayn's companions remained in their belief regarding his imāmate until his death. But they were split, after his death, into three sects:

Those Who Believed in the Imamate of Muḥammad b. al-Ḥanafiyya

One sect believed in the imāmate of Muḥammad b. al-Ḥanafīyya. They claimed that, after the death of al-Ḥasan and al-Ḥusayn, no one alive was closer to the Commander of the Faithful, peace be upon him, than Muḥammad b. al-Ḥanafīyya. Therefore, he was the most eligible person for the imāmate, like al-Ḥusayn was more eligible for it, after al-Ḥasan, than the latter's sons. Hence, Muḥammad is the imām after al-Ḥusayn.

The Mukhtārīyya

Another sect said that Muḥammad b. al-Ḥanafīyya, may Allāh, the Exalted, have mercy on his soul, is al-Mahdī, and he was the heir of ʿAlī b. Abī Ṭālib, peace be upon him. No one of his household was permitted to oppose him, dispute his imāmate, or use the sword without his permission. They said that al-Ḥasan b. ʿAlī fought against Muʿāwiya with the permission of Muḥammad and made the truce with his permission too. Al-Ḥusayn too, they said, fought Yazīd with his permission; otherwise, both [al-Ḥasan and al-Ḥusayn] would be misguided and would perish, for anyone who opposes Muḥammad b. al-Ḥanafīyya is blasphemous. They also said that he appointed al-Mukhtār b. Abī ʿUbayda al-Thaqafī governor on Kūfa and Baṣra after the death of al-Ḥusayn and ordered him to take revenge for his blood and kill those who murdered him and to follow them wherever they might be. He named him "*Kaysān*" for his intellect (*kays*) and his piety. They are called "the Mukhtārīyya and also the ʿAbbāsīyya."

When Muḥammad b. al-Ḥanafīyya died in Medīna in Muharram of the year eighty-one (AH), he was sixty-five years. He lived twenty-four years during his father's life and forty-one years after his father's death. His mother was Khawlah bt. Jaʿfar b. Qays b. Maslama b. ʿUbayd b. Yarbūʿ b. Thaʿlaba b. ad-Duʾl b. Ḥanīfa b. Taym b. ʿAlī b. Bakr b. Wāʾil; and Muḥammad took his last name from her tribe. His followers were divided into three sects after his death:

The Karbīyya

One sect said that Muḥammad b. al-Ḥanafīyya was al-Mahdī and that ʿAlī, peace be upon him, named him al-Mahdī and that he did not die and will not die because he is immortal; but he disappeared to an unknown place. He will come back, they said, and will rule the world, and there is no imām between his disappearance and his return. These were the followers of Ibn Karb and they were called "the Karbīyya." Ḥamza b. ʿUmārah al-Barbari was one of them. He was from Medīna. Then he deviated from this sect, claiming that he was a prophet and that Muḥammad b. al-Ḥanafīyya is Allāh – Allāh is certainly Exalted and dissociated from this claim. He also claimed that he [i.e. Ḥamza] was the imām and that he had seven powers (*asbāb*) from Heaven that would enable him to conquer and rule the world. Many people from Medīna and Kūfa followed him. Abū Jaʿfar, Muḥammad b. ʿAlī b. al-Ḥusayn, peace be upon him, cursed him and dissociated himself from him and called him a liar, and so did the Shīʿa. Two men from [the tribe of] Nahd followed his claim, one was called Ṣāʿid[1] and the other was called Bayān.[2] The latter was a hay merchant from Kūfa. He claimed that Muḥammad b. ʿAlī b. al-Ḥusayn appointed him. Khālid b. ʿAbdillāh al-Qasrī[3] arrested him along with fifteen of his followers and tied them to reed bundles, then poured fuel on them and set them on fire in the mosque of Kūfa. One of them released himself, but when he looked back and saw his comrades on fire, he

---

[1] Ṣāʾid al-Nahdī was cursed by Jaʿfar al-Ṣādiq, who called him a liar and asked people not to believe his claims.

[2] Bayān b. Samʿān al-Tamīmī al-Nahdī (d. 119 AH) started his movement in Iraq during the first quarter of the second century (AH). He ended up claiming that he was a prophet. Khālid al-Qasrī captured him and ordered that he be killed and crucified.

[3] Khālid al-Qasrī (d. 126 AH) was the governor of both Kūfa and Baṣra. His position was given to Yūsuf b. ʿUmar al-Thaqafī in 120 AH.

jumped back and was burned with them. Ḥamza b. ʿUmāra [al-Barbari] married his own daughter and permitted all non-permissible deeds, claiming that a person who knows the imām can do whatever he pleases without fearing guilt. The followers of Ibn Karb, Ṣāʾid, and Bayān are waiting for their return and claim that Muḥammad b. al-Ḥanafīyya will re-appear after having been in hiding from the people; and he will come to this life and become the Commander of the Faithful. This was the last of their account.

Another sect said that Muḥammad b. al-Ḥanafīyya did not die, but he is residing in the Raḍwā Mountains, between Mecca and Medīna, being fed and cared for by the milk and meat of gazelles. There is a lion on each side of his seat to protect him until he returns to rule. Some of them said that there is a lion on the right and a tiger on the left. According to this sect, he is the expected imām, who was mentioned by the Prophet, peace be upon him, and his family, and that he will fill the world with justice and fairness. They remained on this belief until they perished, except for a few of them remaining until now. These are one of the ʿAbbāsīyya sects.

One of the ʿAbbāsīyya men was al-Sayyid Ismāʿīl b. Muḥammad b. Yazīd b. Rabīʿa b. Mufarrigh al-Ḥimyarī,[1] the poet. He said:

O Raḍwā Mountain! Why is your resident not seen?
Until when are you in hiding, yet so close?

---

[1] Al-Sayyid a-Ḥimyarī (d. 137 AH) was one of the main Shīʿite poets in the Umayyad period. Most of his poetry was dedicated to the cause of the family of the Prophet.

O Son of the Heir, who was named after Muḥammad!
My soul is melting for your sake
Even if he were absent for the age of Noah
Our souls are certain of his return

He also said about him:

Greet the resident of Raḍwā Mountain,
and send to his home your *Salaam*
Some of us, loyal to you, were hurt,
since they called you the *Imām*
They combated, for you, all people on earth,
for the seventy years of your absence
He remained in the Mount of Raḍwā
Angels are speaking with him
The son of Khawlah has not tasted death,
nor has the ground covered his bones

Some people said that al-Sayyid [Ismāʿīl] b. Muḥammad rescinded his position and believed in the imāmate of Jaʿfar b. Muḥammad,[1] pace be upon him. He wrote a poem about his repentance that begins with:

I became a *Jaʿfari* (*tajaʿfartu*) in the name of Allāh,
and Allāh is Great

Al-Sayyid was also called "Abū Hāshim."

---

[1] Jaʿfar al-Ṣādiq (d. 148 AH) is the sixth Imām of the Twelver Shīʿa. He was a highly distinguished jurist. Among his students are Abū Ḥanīfa and Mālik, who founded their own schools of jurisprudence, and Jābir b. Ḥayyān, the father of chemistry.

Those Who Believed in the Imamate of Abū Hāshim (The Hāshimīyya)

Another sect said that Muḥammad b. al-Ḥanafīyya did die and the imām after him is ʿAbdullāh b. Muḥammad, his son.[1] He was called "Abū Hāshim" and he was his father's oldest son. His father designated him for succession. This sect was named "the Hāshimīyya," after Abū Hāshim.

Another sect said concerning him the like the claims of the ʿAbbāsīyya about his father – that he was al-Mahdī and that he did not die. They also said that he revived the dead and other exaggerations. When Abū Hāshim ʿAbdullāh b. Muḥammad b. al-Ḥanafīyya died, his followers became four sects:

The Pure ʿAbbāsīyya

One sect said that ʿAbdullāh b. Muḥammad died and he designated his brother, ʿAlī b. Muḥammad. His mother was from Quḍāʿah named Umm ʿUthmān bt. Abī Judayr b. ʿAbdah...b. Quḍāʿah. According to them,

[1] Abū Hāshim ʿAbdullāh b. Muḥammad (d. 99 AH) was working to substitute the Umayyad regime with a Shīʿite caliphate. He was poisoned by the Umayyad caliph, Sulaymān b. ʿAbd a-Malik.

those, who claim that he designated Muḥammad b. 'Alī b. 'Abdullāh b. 'Abbās b. 'Abd al-Muṭṭalib,[1] got the names mixed up. Then, they say, 'Alī b. Muḥammad designated his son al-Ḥasan, whose mother was a captive, and he in turn designated his own son, 'Alī b. al-Ḥasan, whose mother was Lubānah bt. Abū Hāshim 'Abdullāh b. Muḥammad b. al-Ḥanafīyya. 'Alī b. al-Ḥasan then designated his own son al-Ḥasan b. 'Alī, whose mother is 'Ulayyah bt. 'Awn b. 'Alī b. Muḥammad b. al-Ḥanafīyya. According to this sect, the imāmate belongs to the descendents of Muḥammad b. al-Ḥanafīyya and it cannot be transferred to others, and al-Mahdī will be one of them. These sects are "the pure 'Abbāsīyya," who retained this name, and this particular sect is called the Mukhtārīyya. But a sect emerged from them terminating the imāmate of this line and saying that al-Ḥasan died without designating anyone, so there is no imām or heir after him until the return of Muḥammad b. al-Ḥanafīyya, who will be al-Mahdī.

The Ḥārithīyya

Another sect said that Abū Hāshim 'Abdullāh b. Muḥammad b. al-Ḥanafīyya designated 'Abdullāh b.

[1] Abū 'Abdullāh Muḥammad b. 'Alī b. 'Abdullāh b. al-'Abbās (d.126 AH) was the father of the first two 'Abbāsid caliphs – as-Saffāḥ and al-Manṣūr. He transferred his claim for the imāmate to his son, Ibrāhīm al-Imām, who transferred it to his own brother as-Saffāḥ.

Muʿāwiya b. ʿAbdullāh b. Jaʿfar b. Abī Ṭālib,[1] who revolted in Kūfa. His mother is Umm ʿAwn bt. ʿAwn b. al-ʿAbbās b. Rabīʿa b. al-Ḥārith b. ʿAbd al-Muṭṭalib. Since he was a juvenile, he trusted Ṣāliḥ b. Mudrik – as a regent – until ʿAbdullāh b. Muʿāwiya reached the right age to become the imām who knew everything. They exaggerated in their claims, going as far as saying that Allāh, the Exalted, is light, which emanates from ʿAbdullāh b. Muʿāwiya. This sect is named "the Ḥārithyya," the followers of ʿAbdullāh b. al-Ḥārith, who came from al-Madāʾin. All of them are *Ghulāt* (extremists). They used to say, "He who knows the imām can do whatever he wants." ʿAbdullāh b. Muʿāwiya revolted in Iṣfahān, and he was killed in jail by Abū Muslim.[2]

[1] ʿAbdullāh b. Muʿāwiya (d. 129 AH) revolted in Kūfa in 127 AH. He managed to threaten the Umayyad rule for two years. He was finally defeated by the Umayyad army and was compelled to escape to Hirāt. Its governor jailed him and he was killed at the orders of Abū Muslim al-Khurāsānī.

[2] Abū Muslim al-Khurāsānī (d. 137 AH) was the real founder of the ʿAbbāsid regime. He led the forces that toppled the Umayyad rule and installed Abū al-ʿAbbās as-Saffāḥ in the position of the caliphate. He remained loyal to him and to his brother Abū Jaʿfar al-Manṣūr until no enemies were left for al-Manṣūr to worry about. At that time, al-Manṣūr killed him. His followers were called "the Abū Muslimiyya."

THE SHIʿA DIVERGENCE AFTER THE ASSASSINATION OF ʿALĪ

The Rāwandīyya Extremists (*ghulāt*)

Another sect said that ʿAbdullāh b. Muḥammad b. al-Ḥanafīyya designated Muḥammad b. ʿAlī b. ʿAbdullāh b. al-ʿAbbās b. ʿAbd al-Muṭṭalib, because he died in Syria and designated, as a regent, ʿAlī b. ʿAbdullāh b. al-ʿAbbās whose son, Muḥammad, was young when Abū Hāshim died. He ordered him to deliver the imāmate to his son when he reached the age of adulthood, for he is the imām and he is Allāh, the Exalted, who knows everything and whoever knows him can do as he pleases. These are the Rāwandīyya *Ghulāt*. After a dispute between the followers of ʿAbdullāh b. Muʿāwiya and the followers of Muḥammad b. ʿAlī about the heir of Abū Hāshim, they agreed to ask one of their learned leaders, named Abū Riyāḥ. He testified that Abū Hāshim ʿAbdullāh b. Muḥammad b. al-Ḥanafīyya designated Muḥammad b. ʿAlī b. al-ʿAbbās. Most of the followers of ʿAbdullāh b. Muʿāwiya joined the believers in the imāmate of Muḥammad b. ʿAlī and the Rāwandīyya became stronger by this gain.

The Bayānīyya

Another sect said that al-Mahdī is Abū Hāshim, the ruler of all the people. He will return to handle people's affairs and rule the world, and he has no heir. They exaggerated in describing him. These are the Bayānīyya, followers of Bayān al-Nahdi. They said that Abū Hāshim is a prophet from Allāh, the Exalted, and Bayān is a prophet as well, citing the Qurʾānic verse: "This is a clear statement (*bayān*) to men and a guidance" (Qurʾān, 3:138). Bayān claimed prophethood after the death of Abū Hāshim and wrote a letter to Abū Jaʿfar[1] Muḥammad b. ʿAlī b. al-Ḥusayn, peace be upon him, asking him to acknowledge his Prophethood saying: "Submit so that you may survive and ascend a ladder, and prosper. For you do not know where Allāh places prophethood and His message. Certainly the Messenger's task is only the delivery of the Message; and he, who warns, is blameless." Abū Jaʿfar, peace be upon him, ordered the carrier of his letter – a man named ʿUmar b. ʿAfīf al-Azdī – to eat it. Bayān was killed while maintaining this claim.

[1] Abū Jaʿfar Muḥammad al-Bāqir (d. 114 AH) is the fifth imām of the Twelver Shīʿa. He was called "al-Bāqir" because of his deep knowledge.

The Divergence After ʿAbdullāh b. Muʿāwiya

When Abū Muslim killed ʿAbdullāh b. Muʿāwiya in his jail, the latter's sect was divided into three sects. At that time, certain deviant Shīʿa groups joined ʿAbdullāh b. Muʿāwiya, and they were led by a man from his followers named ʿAbdullāh b. al-Ḥārith. His father was a heretic (*zindīq*) from al-Madā'in. He led the followers of ʿAbdullāh b. Muʿāwiya to extremism (*ghuluw*) and the belief in metempsychosis and the "shadows" and "levels," attributing all of these doctrines to Jābir b. ʿAbdillāh al-Anṣārī,[1] then to Jābir b. Yazīd al-Juʿfī.[2] He deceived them and lured them to abandon all religious laws and obligations, claiming that this was the doctrine of Jābir b. ʿAbdillāh and Jābir b. Yazīd, may Allāh be please with them. Indeed they had no such doctrines.

Another sect claimed that ʿAbdullāh b. Muʿāwiya did not die; and that he is living in the mountains of Iṣfahān. They claimed that he will not die before forcing people to submit to a man from Banū Hāshim – from the descendents of ʿAlī and Fāṭima.

---

[1] Jābir b. ʿAbdillāh al-Anṣārī (d. 78 AH) was an eminent companion of the Prophet. He participated in nineteen battles on the Prophet's side. His name continuously appears in Shīʿite transmission of Ḥadīth.

[2] Jābir al-Juʿfī (d. 128 AH) was one of the Shīʿite jurists. He was a follower of al-Ṣādiq and al-Bāqir.

Another sect said that ʿAbdullāh b. Muʿāwiya is al-Mahdī, who was mentioned by the Prophet, peace be upon him, and his family, and that he will rule the world, filling it with fairness and justice after it has been filled with injustice and oppression. Then, when he dies, he will leave his place to a man from Banū Hāshim – from the descendents of ʿAlī b. Abī Ṭālib.

Another sect said that ʿAbdullāh b. Muʿāwiya died without designating anyone for his place, and there is no imām after him. They went astray and became dispersed among the types and sects of the Shīʿa, not guided by anyone. Therefore, all sects of the ʿAbbāsīyya have no imām, but they wait for the dead, except for the ʿAbbāsīyya, who claimed the imāmate for the descendents of al-ʿAbbās and supported them until this day. These are the sects of the ʿAbbāsīyya and the ʿAbbāsīyya and the Ḥārithīyya. From them emerged the sects of Khurramdīnīyya, who gave rise to extreme doctrines (*ghulu*) such as claiming that the imāms are gods and prophets and angels. They are also the ones who believed in the abstractions (*aẓilla*)[1] and metempsychosis and spirits, in addition to speaking about the existence a cycle of many worlds in this world (*dawr*)[2] and denying the Day of

[1] The term *aẓilla* refers to the domain of abstractions, which are entities and non-entities at the same time (like shadows). Everything in that domain has no material body.

[2] This doctrine claims that all world affairs are based on a cycle of causes and effects, which keeps moving on the same track and coming back after the completion of every cycle. There is no consensus, however, on the number of years in the grand

Judgment and Resurrection. They claimed that there is only this world and the Resurrection means the departure of the spirit from one body and its entrance in another – good to good and evil to evil. It is their belief that they are rewarded or tormented in these bodies, because these bodies are either Paradise or Hell. They believe that they are contained in the good bodies during their life and when they are tormented, they will inhabit the ugly bodies of dogs, monkeys, pigs, snakes, scorpions, and beetles – moving from one body to another in eternal torment. For these bodies, they say, are their Hell and Heaven, and there is no Day of Judgment, Resurrection, Paradise or Hell other than what was mentioned. Their bodies deteriorate and perish proportionately to their sins and acts and their denial of their imāms. These bodies, which are their homes, vanish and the spirits move on to other bodies, or to ones of the tormented [animal] bodies. This is the meaning of the return for them, while the bodies are only dwellings furnished by people and, when they are abandoned, they become ruins; or like dresses, which people wear and throw away, when they become worn and faded, and wear new ones. They say that reward and punishment touches the spirits and not the bodies, citing Allāh's statement, "He formed you in whatever image he willed." (Qur'ān, 82:8) and His statement, "There is not an animal on earth, nor a being that flies with [the help of] its wings, but communities like you." (Qur'ān, 6:38) and His statement, "There never was a people without a warner." (Qur'ān, 35:24) All flying beings, animals, and

---

cycle (*al-Dawrat al-Kubrā*); most of them settle for thirty thousand years (See *al-Milal wa al-Niḥal*, p. 714-16).

wild beasts were, therefore, communities of people who received warners sent by Allāh. Those who were good, their spirits are transferred, after the ruin of the bodies, to other good bodies in order to be dignified and rewarded; and the spirits of evil ones were moved to evil and ugly bodies to be tormented in this world. They were given the worst forms, the nastiest and filthiest foods. They cited in support of this claim the statement of Allāh, the Exalted, "As for man, when his God tries him and gives him honor and bounty, he says: 'My God honored me;' but when He tries him and restricts his subsistence, then he says: 'My God has humiliated me.'" (Qurʾān, 89:15-16) But Allāh, the Exalted, uncovers the lies of such people and refutes their claim, because they disobeyed Him. He says, "Nay, but you do not honor the orphan," (Qurʾān, 89:17). He refers to the Prophet, peace be upon him, and his family. "Nor do you encourage one another to feed the poor," (Qurʾān, 89:18), meaning the imām. "And you devour inheritance – all with greed," (Qurʾān, 89:19) meaning that you do not give the imām his right from what He [i.e. Allāh] endowed you with.

The Manṣūrīyya

Another sect was called the Manṣūrīyya, the followers of Abū Manṣūr, who claimed that Allāh, the Exalted, lifted him to His side and brought him very close to Him and passed His hand on his head and said (in Syriac), "O My son!" He claimed that he is a prophet and that Allāh chose him for a confidant. This particular Abū Manṣūr was a man from Kūfa, from the tribe of ʿAbd al-Qays. He had a house there, but he grew up in the desert. He was illiterate, but he claimed after the death of Abū Jaʿfar Muḥammad b. ʿAlī b. al-Ḥusayn, peace be upon him, that Abū Jaʿfar designated him as his heir. Then he went as far as claiming that ʿAlī b. Abī Ṭālib, peace be upon him, was a prophet, as well as al-Ḥasan, al-Ḥusayn, and Muḥammad b. al-Ḥanafīyya, and he also is a prophet; then the prophethood will belong to six of his own descendants – the last of whom is al-Qāʾim. He was commanding his followers to strangle to death or assassinate anyone, who opposed them, saying: "Anyone who opposes you is a blasphemer. Kill him, for this is the covert *jihād*. He also claimed that Gabriel, peace be upon him, brings him revelation from Allāh, the Exalted; and that Allāh, the Exalted, sent Muḥammad with the Qurʾān and He sent him with the interpretation thereof. Khālid b. ʿAbdullāh al-Qasrī went after him, but he failed to capture him.[1] But ʿUmar al-Khannāq captured his son, al-Ḥusayn b. Abī Manṣūr, after claiming the prophethood to succeed his father and beginning to receive large sums of money and acquiring many supporters, who believed in his prophethood. He was sent to al-Mahdī [the ʿAbbāsid caliph], who killed and crucified him – after he confessed – and confiscated a lot of money from him. Then he chased his followers and captured some of them, then killed and crucified them as well.

These are the extremists, followers of ʿAbdullāh b. Muʿāwiya and the ʿAbbāsid Rāwandīyya – among others. However, the followers of ʿAbdullāh b. Muʿāwiya claim

[1] Yūsuf b. ʿUmar al-Thaqafī, the governor of Kūfa and Baṣra, captured him and ordered him to be killed and crucified.

that they recognize one another as they relocate from one body to another since they were in the Ark with Noah and every prophet through the ages. They also call themselves by the names of the Companions of the Prophet, peace be upon him, and his family, claiming that their [i.e. the Companions'] spirits are in their bodies. They cite the statement of ʿAlī b. Abī Ṭālib, peace be upon him, which was also attributed to the Prophet, peace be upon him, and his family: "the spirits are like soldiers, the ones that recognize each other live in harmony, while the ones that fail to recognize each other remain at odds." They say, "We recognize one another in the same way described by the Prophet, peace be upon him, and his family." They also believed in metempsychosis and relocation of spirits for certain periods of time. Faithful spirits move from human bodies to animals, for pastime, like horses and the other mounts of kings and caliphs – proportionately with their religiosity and obedience to their imāms. They will be treated well, fed well, and clothed well – admirable, clean, and expensive saddles will be placed on them. Spirits of moderate faith would go to animals that belong to moderate people. This relocation will last for one thousand years, before a new relocation to human bodies occurs and lasts for the following ten thousand years. This is a test of humility, so they retain their obedience and acquire no vanity. As to blasphemous, polytheist, hypocrite, and disobedient spirits, they relocate to ugly bodies for [ten] thousand years relocating from elephants and camels to extremely tiny gnats. They cite the statement of Allāh, the Exalted, "[and they will not enter the Paradise] until the camel can pass through the eye of a needle." (Qurʾān: 7:40) They said, "We know the size of a camel as we know that a creature of this size can never pass from the eye of a needle. And since Allāh's statement can not be a lie, the only way for a camel to pass is by the reduction of its size and the gradual shrinkage in every cycle (*dawr*) until an elephant and a camel become in the size of a gnat and pass through the eye of a needle. When it passes from the eye of a needle, it will return to a human body for another thousand years. Indeed, it will be placed in a weak and needy body that needs to perform hard work and endure hardship in seeking subsistence. Some will be tanners and others will work in cupping, or street cleaning, while others will perform other hard, dirty, and repulsive works, depending on the type of their sins. They will be tested in these bodies by being asked to believe in the imāms and the prophets and messengers. They will not believe in, or recognize, any of them. Indeed, they will accuse them of lying. Therefore, they will relocate from one human body to another for a thousand years, after which they will return to their first torment for ten thousand years. This is their eternal condition and this is the Resurrection and Judgment, and the Hell and the Paradise." This is their doctrine on the Return (*al-Raj'ah*):[1] there is no return to this life after death; all bodies perish and vanish without return.

[1] The Return (*al-Raj'ah*) is the return of certain people after their death and before the Day of Judgment. The opponents of Shī'ism consider this doctrine an innovation. Those who believe in it claim that 'Alī b. Abī Ṭālib and his sons will return to life in order to get even with their enemies – who will also return to life.

The Rāwandīyya[1] and the Mughīrīyya, followers of al-Mughīra b. Saʿīd,[2] said, "We do not deny that Allāh has omnipotence. Therefore, we do not believe in the Return, nor do we dispute it. If Allāh, the Exalted wanted to make it happen, He would."

The ʿAbbāsīyya said that people will return in their original bodies and Muḥammad, peace be upon him, and his family, and all other prophets, who will believe in him. And ʿAlī b. Abī Ṭālib will return and kill Muʿāwiya b. Abī Sufyān and all the family of Abī Sufyān, then he will destroy Damascus and flood [the city of] Baṣra.

The Khaṭṭābīyya

The followers of Abū al-Khaṭṭāb,[3] Muḥammad b. Abī Zaynab al-Ajdaʿ al-Asadī, and their supporters became

---

[1] The text has "al-Zaydiyya," which is not correct. The Zaydiyya unequivocally deny the Return (*al-Rajʿah*). See *al-Munya wa al-Amal*, p. 87.

[2] Al-Mughīra b. Saʿīd al-ʿIjlī (d. 119 AH) started spreading his teaching in Kūfa during the reign of Khālid al-Qasrī, who captured him and ordered him to be killed and burnt. Al-Shahrastānī called him al-Bajalī (*Milal*, p. 180), while Ibn Ḥazm said that he was a *mawlā* of the Bajīla tribe (*Fasl* II, p. 114).

[3] He was captured and killed in 143 AH. Not much is known about his life. He will be mentioned again when the author describes the doctrines of his sect, the Khaṭṭābiyya.

divided when they knew that Abū ʿAbdullāh, Jaʿfar b. Muḥammad, peace be upon them, cursed [Abū al-Khaṭṭāb] and dissociated himself from him and his followers. Abū al-Khaṭṭāb claimed that Abū ʿAbdullāh, Jaʿfar b. Muḥammad, peace be upon them, appointed him as his representative and heir, after him, and taught him Allāh's greatest name. Then, he claimed to be a prophet, then an angel. He finally claimed to be Allāh's messenger to all people and the witness over them. His followers became four sects:

One sect said that that Abū ʿAbdullāh, Jaʿfar b. Muḥammad, is Allāh, the Exalted – Allāh is certainly above that. They also claimed that Abū al-Khaṭṭāb is a prophet sent by Jaʿfar, who ordered them to obey him. They permitted unlawful conduct, like adultery, stealing, and intoxication. They also cancelled the alms, prayers, fasting, and the Hajj, and allowed all pleasures for each other. They said if any of them asks his *brother* to testify in his favor, the latter must do so, because it is his duty. They named all duties after certain men, and did the same with vile acts. For permitting the types of unlawful conduct, they cite the statement of Allāh, the Exalted, "Allāh wants to lighten your burden." (Qurʾān: 4:28) They said, "He lightened our burden by [sending] Abū al-Khaṭṭāb and broke our chains and cuffs," meaning prayers, the alms, fasting, and the Hajj. They said, "Whoever knows the prophet-imām can do as he pleases."

Another sect said that Buzaygh[1] is a prophet sent by Jaʿfar b. Muḥammad, like Abū al-Khaṭṭāb. While Buzaygh acknowledged the prophethood of Abū al-Khaṭṭāb, the latter and his followers did not reciprocate. They dissociated themselves from Buzaygh.

Another sect said that al-Sariy[2] is a prophet, like Abū al-Khaṭṭāb, sent by Jaʿfar, who said that he is strong and honest and he is Moses, the strong and honest. They said that he has the same spirit [of Moses]. According to them, Jaʿfar is Islam, and Islam is peace (*salām*), and Peace is Allāh, the Exalted. "We are the sons of Islam," they said – like the Jews, who said: "We are the sons of Allāh and His beloved." (Qurʾān, 5:18). The Prophet, peace be upon him, and his family, said, "Salmān is the son of Islam." They advocated the prophethood of al-Sariy, while praying, fasting, and performing Ḥajj to Jaʿfar b. Muḥammad, saying: "*Labbayka yā Jaʿfar! Labbayk!*"[3]

Another sect said that Jaʿfar b. Muḥammad, is Allāh, the Exalted – Allāh is certainly above that. They said, "He is light that enters the bodies of the heirs (*awṣiyāʾ*) and unites with them. The light was in Jaʿfar, then exited from him and entered Abū al-Khaṭṭāb. Then Jaʿfar be-

---

[1] Buzaygh b. Mūsā claimed that some of his followers are better than the angels. Imām Jaʿfar al-Ṣādiq cursed him and called him a liar.

[2] Al-Sariy al-Aqṣam was also cursed by Imām Jaʿfar al-Ṣādiq, along with Bayān and Buzaygh.

[3] Originally, it is the call of Muslim pilgrims during the *Ḥajj*. They say "*Labbayka Allāhumma Labbayk!*" They address Allah, the Exalted, and show their obedience in answering His call.

came one of the angels. The light then exited from Abū al-Khaṭṭāb and entered the body of Maʿmar and Abū al-Khaṭṭāb became an angel, while Maʿmar is Allāh, the Exalted. Then Ibn al-Labbān began to call for believing in Maʿmar, saying that he is Allāh, the Exalted, and to him he prayed and fasted. He permitted all pleasures, saying, "Allāh created them for His servants. How can they be unlawful?" He permitted adultery; stealing; intoxication; consumption of blood, dead animals, and the meat of pigs; marrying one's mother, daughter, or sister; and sex among men. He also abolished washing one's body after sexual intercourse (*ghusl al-Janābah*), saying, "Why wash from a sperm, of which I was created?" He claimed that anything that was prohibited by the Qurʾān must be a name of a certain man. Some Shīʿa disputed their argument saying, "Those you claim to be angels have dissociated themselves from Maʿmar and Buzaygh and said they are two devils and cursed them." They said, "The ones you see in the image of Jaʿfar and Abū al-Khaṭṭāb are two devils, who impersonate Jaʿfar and Abū al-Khaṭṭāb, to divert the people from the truth. But in reality, Jaʿfar and Abū al-Khaṭṭāb are two grand angels near the greatest God, the God of Heaven, while Maʿmar is the God of earth, who obeys the God of Heaven and knows his virtues and status." They asked them, "How can this be, and Muḥammad, peace be upon him, and his family, used to acknowledge that he was the servant of Allāh, and that his God – the God of all creatures – is one and He is Allāh, the Lord of Heaven and Earth, and no other god exists?" They replied, "When Muḥammad, peace be upon him, and his family, said this, he was a servant and a messenger sent by Abū Ṭālib.[1] The light that is Allāh was in ʿAbd al-Muṭṭalib[2] and went to Abū Ṭālib and then went to Muḥammad, and from him moved to ʿAlī b. Abī Ṭālib, peace be upon him. Therefore, all of them are gods." They asked them, "How can this be, and Muḥammad, peace be upon him, and his family, asked Abū Ṭālib to accept Islam and faith and the latter declined? The Prophet, peace be upon him, and his family, then said, "I will request him from my God and he will grant my request." They said, "Muḥammad and Abū Ṭālib were mocking the people. For Allāh, the Exalted, said: 'They ridicule them, Allāh will ridicule them' (Qur'ān, 9:79) and Abū Ṭālib is Allāh, the Exalted." Allāh is certainly above that. They go on to say, "When Abū Ṭālib died, the spirit exited his body to Muḥammad, peace be upon him, and his family, and he became Allāh, the Exalted, in reality, and ʿAlī the Prophet. When Muḥammad, peace be upon him, and his family, died, the spirit exited his body and went to ʿAlī. It continued its incarnation – from one to another – until it reached Maʿmar."

---

[1] Abū Ṭālib (d. 3 B.H.) is the Prophet's uncle and the father of Imām ʿAlī. He protected the Prophet from the harm of his opponents when Islam was still vulnerable. His death left the Prophet susceptible to all kinds of harm, which he avoided only by leaving Mecca.

[2] ʿAbd al-Muṭṭalib is the Prophet's grandfather. The Prophet was born an orphan, so ʿAbd al-Muṭṭalib was in charge of raising him.

THE DIVERGENCE AFTER ʿABDULLĀH B. MUʿĀWĪYYA

These are the sects of extremism (*ghuluw*), who styled themselves as part of the Shīʿa. They all belong to the Khurramdīnīyya,[1] the Zindīqīyya,[2] the Dahrīyya[3] – may Allāh curse them all. All of them agree on denying Allāh, the Exalted Creator, as God. Instead, they worship certain created bodies. They claim that the body is Allāh's home and that Allāh, the Exalted, is light and spirit that moves in these bodies – Allāh is certainly highly above what they claim. However, they diverge in their loyalties to their chiefs. The also denounce each other and curse one another.

---

[1] The name "Khurramdīniyya" is made of two Persian words, *Khurram* (pleasurable) and *Dīn* (religion). Therefore, as a religious doctrine, it refers to directing people to follow pleasures and abandon religious obligations.

[2] The Zindīqiyya are the Dualists. Those who were charged with belonging to this sect were condemned to death. Such charges became a convenient tool to eliminate the enemies during the ʿAbbāsid era.

[3] The doctrine of the Dahriyya rests on denying a creator. The origin of this belief predates Islam. It is disputed by the Qurʾān (45:24), "They said it is only this life; we die and live; nothing but time (*dahr*) cause us to die; they have no certain knowledge about this; indeed, they only conjecture."

The ʿAbbāsid Shīʿa

The ʿAbbāsid Shīʿa, the Rāwandīyya, split into three sects:

The Abū-Muslimīyya

One sect is called the Abū-Muslimīyya, followers of Abū Muslim [al-Khurāsānī], who believed in his imāmate and claimed that he did not die. They allowed all of the impermissible acts and abandoned all religious obligations. They said that faith is nothing more than knowing their imām. They were called the Khurramdīnīyya. The Khurramīyya emerged from this sect.

The Rizāmīyya

Another sect remained loyal to their ancestors and maintained loyalty to Abū Muslim. They are called the Rizāmīyya, followers of Rizām.[1] Their origin goes back to the ʿAbbāsīyya.

---

[1] Not much is known about Rizām, except for his doctrine confirming the death of Abū Muslim al-Khurāsānī. (*Firaq*, p. 256-7; *Maqālāt Al-Islāmiyīn* I, p. 94; *Milal*, p. 152)

THE DIVERGENCE AFTER 'ABDULLĀH B. MU'ĀWĪYYA

The Hurayrīyya

Another sect called the Hurayrīyya, followers of Abū Hurayra al-Rāwandī. These are the pure 'Abbāsīyya, who said that the imāmate belonged to al-'Abbās,[1] may Allāh be pleased with him, the uncle of the Prophet, peace be upon him, and his family. They continued, in secret, to be loyal to their ancestors – not willing to accuse them of blasphemy – and, yet, remained also loyal to Abū Muslim, whom they held in high esteem. This sect had extreme exaggerations about al-'Abbās and his descendents.

Another sect said that Muḥammad b. al-Ḥanafīyya was the imām after his father, 'Alī b. Abī Ṭālib. When he died, he designated his son, Abū Hāshim 'Abdullāh b. Muḥammad; and the latter designated Muḥammad b. 'Alī b. al-'Abbās b. 'Abd al-Muṭṭalib, because he died near him in Syria. Muḥammad b. 'Alī designated his own son, Ibrāhīm b. Muḥammad, also called al-Imām,[2] who was the first among the descendents of al-'Abbās to be designated for the imāmate, and Abū Muslim [al-Khurāsānī] was one of those who supported his imāmate. Then, Ibrāhīm b. Muḥammad designated his brother, Abū al-

---

[1] Al-'Abbās b. 'Abd al-Muṭṭalib is the uncle of the Prophet. He converted to Islam shortly before the Muslims entered Mecca. He is the ancestor of the 'Abbāsid caliphs.

[2] Ibrāhīm al-Imām (d. 131 AH) was the leader of the 'Abbāsid movement. He used the help of Abū Muslim al-Khurāsānī to fight the Umayyads and topple their regime. Marwān b. Muḥammad, the last Umayyad caliph, arrested Ibrāhīm and killed him in prison.

ʿAbbās ʿAbdullāh b. Muḥammad,[1] who was the first among the descendents of al-ʿAbbās to be designated for the imāmate and the caliphate. Abū al-ʿAbbās then designated his brother, Abū Jaʿfar ʿAbdullāh b. Muḥammad, also called al-Manṣūr.[2] Before his death, al-Manṣūr designated his son, al-Mahdī[3] Muḥammad b. ʿAbdullāh.[4] The latter changed the belief, of this sect, about the imāmate of Muḥammad b. al-Ḥanafīyya and his son Abū Hāshim. He claimed that the imāmate after the Prophet, peace be upon him, and his family, went to al-ʿAbbās b.

---

[1] Abū al-ʿAbbās As-Saffāḥ (d. 136 AH) was the first ʿAbbāsid caliph. He was appointed for the caliphate in Kūfa in 132 AH, after the demise of the Umayyad regime. He was called Al-Saffāḥ (the Shedder of Blood) because of his cruelty and love for killing. He died at the age of thirty-two, in his makeshift capital, al-Hāshimiyya, during a chickenpox epidemic.

[2] Abū Jaʿfar al-Manṣūr (d. 158 AH) was the second ʿAbbāsid caliph. He built Baghdad and made it his capital. The duration of his caliphate was twenty-two years, which allowed him to establish his regime and eliminate all enemies, including his former allies – like Abū Muslim al-Khurāsānī.

[3] A distinction must be made between "al-Mahdī," the third ʿAbbāsid caliph, and "al-Mahdī," the hidden imām, who is awaited by the Shīʿa. The former is referred to only in this section of the book. All other occurrences of the name refer to the latter.

[4] Muḥammad b. ʿAbdillāh al-Mahdī (d. 169 AH) was the third ʿAbbāsid caliph. He was designated for the caliphate by his father, al-Manṣūr. He ruled for ten years.

ʿAbd al-Muṭṭalib, saying that al-ʿAbbās was [the Prophet's] uncle and his heir and the closest of people to him. He also said that Abū Bakr, ʿUmar, ʿUthmān, and ʿAlī, peace be upon him, – and all the ones who had the caliphate after the Prophet, peace be upon him, and his family – were usurpers and opportunists. They accepted his argument in acknowledging the imāmate of al-ʿAbbās after the Messenger of Allāh, peace be upon him, and his family. The mother of al-ʿAbbās was Nutayla bt. Janāb b. Kulayb b. Mālik b. ʿAmr b. ʿĀmir b. Zayd b. Manāt b. al-Ḍaḥyān, ʿĀmir b. Saʿd b. al-Khazraj b. Taymullāh b. al-Nimr b. Qāsiṭ. He claimed that, after al-ʿAbbās, the imāmate went to ʿAbdullāh b. al-ʿAbbās,[1] whose mother – and the mother of al-Faḍl, Qutham, and ʿUbaydullāh – was Lubābah bt. al-Ḥārith b. Ḥazn b. Bujayr b. al-Ḥazm b. Ruwayba b. ʿAbdullāh b. Hilāl b. ʿĀmir b. Ṣaʿṣaʿa. Then he claimed the imāmate for ʿAlī b. ʿAbdullāh, also known as al-Sajjād,[2] who was an ascetic. His mother was Zarʿah bt. Shurayh b. Maʿdikarb b. Wulayʿa b. Shuraḥbīl b. ʿAmr b. Muʿāwiya b. al-Ḥārith b. Muʿāwiya b. Kinda. Then he claimed the imāmate for Ibrāhīm b. Muḥammad al-Imām; whose mother was a captive named Fāṭima. Then he claimed the imāmate after Ibrāhīm for his brother, Abdullāh, Abū al-ʿAbbās [al-Saffāh], whose

[1] ʿAbdullāh b. al-ʿAbbās (d. 68 AH) was the Prophet's cousin and companion. He is revered by all Muslims, regardless of their partisanship. He was in the army of ʿAlī in all his battles. He was considered one of the most knowledgeable Muslim jurists.

[2] He is not to be confused with ʿAlī al-Sajjād, the fourth Imām of the Twelver Shīʿa.

mother was Rayṭah bt. ʿUbaydullāh b. ʿAbdullāh b. ʿAbd b. ʿAbdul-Mudān b. al-Dayyān b. Qaṭn b. Ziyād b. al-Ḥārith b. Mālik b. Rabīʿa b. Kaʿb b. al-Ḥārith b. Kaʿb. Then he claimed it for his brother ʿAbdullāh Abū Jaʿfar al-Manṣūr, whose mother was a Berberene captive named Sallāma. Indeed, Abū al-ʿAbbās had designated his brother Abū Jaʿfar as his first heir, and after him, his nephew, ʿĪsā b. Mūsā b. Muḥammad b. ʿAlī b. al-ʿAbbās;[1] but ʿAbdullāh b. ʿAlī b. ʿAbdullāh disagreed with him and claimed the imāmate for himself. Abū Muslim [al-Khurāsānī] fought and defeated him. Then he fled and took refuge in Baṣra. Following an amnesty, he surrendered, but al-Manṣūr killed him later. He had some ties to [ʿAbdullāh] b. al-Muqaffaʿ, the *zindīq*.[2] When al-

[1] ʿĪsā b. Mūsā (d. 167 AH) was the nephew of Al-Saffāḥ and al-Manṣūr. He was the governor of Kūfa and the heir of al-Manṣūr for the caliphate, but al-Manṣūr gave him a large sum of money to yield to al-Manṣūr's son, al-Mahdī. When al-Mahdī became caliph, he virtually eliminated him completely – as al-Nawbakhtī described.

[2] ʿAbdullāh b. al-Muqaffaʿ (d. 142 AH) was one of the masters of eloquence in all times. He was close to both Umayyad and ʿAbbāsid politicians. Among his works are: an Arabic translation of *Kalīla wa Dimna*, *al-Adab al-Kabīr*, and *al-Adab al-Ṣaghīr*. The "ties" between him and ʿAbdullāh b. ʿAlī, to which al-Nawbakhtī refers here, culminated in an amnesty agreement he wrote for ʿAbdullāh b. ʿAlī against any possible betrayal by al-Manṣūr. It stated: "If [al-Manṣūr] betrays his uncle, ʿAbdullāh, then all his women are divorced, all his slaves are free,

Manṣūr's caliphate became stable and his position became firm – after he killed Abū Muslim – his son, Muḥammad b. ʿAbdullāh had already grown up. He named him al-Mahdī and designated him as his heir, pushing aside ʿĪsā b. Mūsā. He placed ʿĪsā after al-Mahdī and gave him twenty thousand Dirhams.

His followers (*shīʿatuhu*) became divided and perplexed and they rejected his conduct, but they refused to give their allegiance to al-Mahdī [son of al-Manṣūr]. They asked their companions, "How can you give your allegiance to al-Mahdī and leave ʿĪsā b. Mūsā, who was designated by Abū al-ʿAbbās to be al-Manṣūr's heir?" They answered, "Complying with the order of the Commander of the Faithful [i.e. al-Manṣūr], who is the imām that must be obeyed according to Allāh's law." They said, "But Abū al-ʿAbbās had to be obeyed too, according to Allāh's law, and he ordered [you] to give your allegiance to Abū Jaʿfar and to ʿĪsā b. Mūsā after Abū Jaʿfar. How could you abandon him and put al-Mahdī ahead of him?" They replied, "Obedience to the imām is mandatory as long as he is alive. Once he dies and another takes his place, the new imām's order is mandatory as long as he lives." They were asked, "What if the Commander of the Faithful, al-Manṣūr, dies, and both al-Mahdī and ʿĪsā b. Mūsā are alive, and the people ignore the order of the Commander of the Faithful, to give their allegiance to al-Mahdī – like

---

and the Muslims have no obligation to obey him (i.e. he would forfeit his rights as a caliph.)" Naturally, al-Manṣūr was not pleased with his attitude, so he asked his governor in Baṣra to deal with him. The most convenient way was to accuse him of being a *zindīq* and kill him for it.

you ignored the order of Abū al-ʿAbbās to give your allegiance to ʿĪsā b. Mūsā? Is this permissible?" They replied, "It is not permissible, after we have already given our allegiance to him." They were asked, "How can it be permissible for you to remove ʿĪsā and support al-Mahdī? Haven't you given your allegiance to him?" They returned to their belief in the imāmate of ʿĪsā b. Mūsā and rejected the imāmate of al-Mahdī. Until this day, they believe that the imāmate belongs to the descendents of ʿĪsā [b. Mūsā]. The Mother of ʿĪsā b. Mūsā was a captive woman. When al-Mahdī was about to die, he designated his son, Mūsā, as his heir, and named him al-Hādī[1], and designated his second son, Hārūn, to be al-Hādī's heir, and named him al-Rashīd.[2] By doing so, he eliminated ʿĪsā totally. The mother of al-Mahdī was named Umm Mūsā bt. Manṣūr b. ʿAbdullāh b. Shimr b. Yazīd b. Wārid b. Maʿdikarb b. al-Wāziʿ...b. Qaydār b. Ismāʿīl b. Ibrāhīm (Abraham).[3] The mother of al-Hādi and al-Rashīd was a captive woman named al-Khayzurān.

---

[1] Mūsā al-Hādi (d. 170 AH) was the fourth ʿAbbāsid caliph. He ruled for a year and was killed after a dispute between him and his mother, al-Khayzurān, about his successor.

[2] Hārūn al-Rashīd (d. 193 AH) is the most famous ʿAbbāsid caliph. He ruled for more than twenty-three years. During his reign, the ʿAbbāsids controlled the largest territory in their history.

[3] By this long and unnecessary list of names, al-Nawbakhtī went out of his way to trace the lineage of this woman all the way to Abraham. Transliterating the whole list does not contribute anything to the argument. It is interesting to see that al-

THE DIVERGENCE AFTER 'ABDULLĀH B. MU'ĀWĪYYA

The Hāshimīyya

Two sects from the 'Abbāsīyya were *Ghulāt*. They exaggerated about the descendents of al-'Abbās, may Allāh's mercy be upon him. One sect was called the Hāshimīyya. They were the followers of Abū Hāshim 'Abdullāh b. Muḥammad b. al-Ḥanafīyya. They said that the imām is knowledgeable; he knows everything and he is in the place of the Prophet, peace be upon him, and his family, in all of his affairs. Whoever does not know him does not know Allāh and, therefore, he is not faithful, but is blasphemous. They transferred the imāmate from Abū Hāshim to the descendents of al-'Abbās.

The Rāwandīyya

Another sect said that the imām knows everything and that he is Allāh, the Exalted (Allāh is certainly above this claim); he brings life and death. They claimed that Abū Muslim was a prophet who could foretell the future. He

---

Nawbakhtī, a Persian, is taking an Arab attitude toward Arab nobility. He insists on providing long lineage for Arab men and women, even those of his opponents; but, when he refers to non-Arab men or women, he simply says: "a *mawlā*," or "a captive woman," followed by the first name only. He does this even when he refers to the mothers of the Imāms, with the sole exception of the mother of Imām 'Alī b. al-Ḥusayn.

was sent by Abū Ja'far al-Manṣūr. These are the Rāwandīyya, the followers of 'Abdullāh al-Rāwandī.[1] They claimed that al-Manṣūr is Allāh (Allāh is certainly above this claim), who knows their secrets and whispers. They declared this claim and, when al-Manṣūr heard about it, he arrested some of them, who admitted their claim. He asked them to repent, but they said, "al-Manṣūr is our god. When he kills us, we become martyrs, like his prophets and messengers, some of whom he killed by the hands of his chosen creatures and some by home destruction, drowning, or wild beasts, while he killed some others by diseases or other ways of his choice. It is up to him to do to his creatures whatever he pleases. He cannot be questioned about his actions."[2] They remained on this belief until this day, claiming that their ancestors held this belief but they could not declare it to the people, which is – according to them – an infraction that will be forgiven by Allāh, but it does not revoke their faith or their obedience for their imām.

---

[1] 'Abdullāh b. Ḥarb al-Kindī al-Kūfī al-Rāwandī (d. 141 AH) was killed, with many of his followers, by al-Manṣūr's general, Ma'n b. Zā'ida al-Shaybānī. Al-Rāzī referred to him as "Abū Hurayra al-Rāwandī (*I'tiqādāt*, p. 95.)

[2] This is a reference to the Qur'ānic verse, "He [i.e. Allah] is not questioned about what He does, but they will be questioned [about their deeds]." (Q, 21:23)

THE DIVERGENCE AFTER ʿABDULLĀH B. MUʿĀWĪYYA

The ʿAlawite Shīʿa

The ʿAlawite Shīʿa were those who said that the imāmate of ʿAlī b. Abī Ṭālib, peace be upon him, was mandated by Allāh and His Messenger, peace be upon him, and his family, and continued to believe in his imāmate and the imāmate of al-Ḥasan after him and then the imāmate of al-Ḥusayn. After the death of al-Ḥusayn, they became several sects. One sect believed in the imāmate of ʿAlī b. al-Ḥusayn,[1] who was called Abū Muḥammad and Abū Bakr – which is his prevalent name. This sect remained believing in his imāmate until he died in Medīna in the month of Muharram, 94 AH. He was fifty-five years old, for he was born in 38 AH. His mother was a captive, whose name is Sulāfeh and she was called Jahānshāh, prior to captivity. She was the daughter of Yazdajurd b. Shahrayār who was the last Sāsānid king.

Another sect said that the imāmate was terminated after al-Ḥusayn, and that only three Imāms were designated by name, by the Messenger of Allāh, peace be upon him, and his family. He made them the rightful successors after him. This sect did not acknowledge the imāmate of anyone after these three.

[1] ʿAlī b. al-Ḥusayn b. ʿAlī b. Abī Ṭālib (d. 94 AH) was the fourth Imām of Twelver Shīʿa. He was also named *Zayn al-ʿĀbidīn* and *as-Sajjād*, because of his devotion to worship.

The Zaydīyya

The Surḥūbīyya

Another sect said that the imāmate after al-Ḥusayn belonged to the sons of al-Ḥasan and al-Ḥusayn specifically, and not to the sons of the rest of the progeny of ʿAlī b. Abī Ṭālib. They [i.e. the sons of al-Ḥasan and al-Ḥusayn] all are equally eligible for the imāmate, so long as the one who claims it seeks it by the use of force. Then, he would be the rightful imām and would acquire the status of ʿAlī b. Abī Ṭālib. His imāmate would be mandated by Allāh, the Exalted, and by His Messenger. His family members and all other people must obey him. Anyone who would not support him would be a blasphemer and would perish. However, any one of [the sons of al-Ḥasan and al-Ḥusayn] who claimed the imāmate while sitting at home, being isolated from people by curtains, was also a blasphemer – he and anyone who believed in his imāmate. This sect was called the Surḥūbīyya, the followers of Abū Khālid al-Wāsiṭī,[1] whose name is Yazīd, and the followers

[1] Abū Khālid al-Wāsiṭī is one of the Zaydiyya chiefs. He was a Kūfan, but moved to the city of Wāsiṭ. He was a contemporary of Zayd and Imām Muḥammad al-Bāqir. Some authors said that his name is ʿAmr, but al-Nawbakhtī said it is "Yazīd." (*Mīzān al-Iʿtidāl* II, 286).

of Fuḍayl b. al-Zubayr al-Rassān[1] and Ziyād b. al-Mundhir, who is called Abū al-Jārūd[2] and was called "Surḥūb" by Muḥammad b. ʿAlī b. al-Ḥusayn b. ʿAlī, who said that Surḥūb is a blind demon living in the sea. Abū al-Jārūd was blind at heart and eyes. This sect converged with the two sects that believed in the superiority of ʿAlī over all people after the Prophet, peace be upon him, and his family. All of them supported Zayd b. ʿAlī b. al-Ḥusayn when he revolted in Kūfa. They believed in his imāmate and they were called al-Zaydīyya, but they differ with each other about the Qurʾān, jurisprudence, and religious laws.

The Surḥūbīyya sect said that all prohibitions and permissions are the prerogatives of the family of Muḥammad, peace be upon him, and his family, and the laws are their laws, because they possess all the teachings of the Prophet, peace be upon him, and his family. It is possessed in its entirety by their elders as well as their youth. According to this sect, the youth and the old [of this family] are equals in their knowledge, whether they are in the cradle or in an advanced age.

Some of them held that anyone who claimed that an infant of this Family did not have the same level of knowledge as the Messenger of Allāh, peace be upon him, and his family, was a blasphemer, since none of them needs to learn from anyone, because knowledge grows in

---

[1] Fuḍayl b. al-Zubayr al-Rassān is one of the supporters of Zayd b. ʿAlī. However, al-Ṭūsī says that he is one of the followers of Imām al-Ṣādiq. (*Rijāl al-Kashshī*, p. 217)

[2] Abū al-Jārūd, Ziyād b. Abī Ziyād (d. ca. 150 AH) was called Surḥūb. The Surḥūbiyya sect was named after him.

their hearts in the same way that the rain causes plants to grow. Allāh, the Exalted, taught them, through His kindness, as He wanted. This sect made this argument to avoid admitting that the imāmate belongs exclusively to some members of this family, which would lead to the refutation of their doctrine – that all of them are equal in their eligibility for the imāmate. Nevertheless, they do not attribute to any member of this Family any useful knowledge, other than that which they attribute to Abū Jaʿfar Muḥammad b. ʿAlī and Abū ʿAbdullāh Jaʿfar b. Muḥammad, and only few statements to Zayd b. ʿAlī and very few statements to ʿAbdullāh b. al-Ḥasan al-Maḥḍ.[1] Indeed, they have nothing but false claims, because they described all the members of this family as being knowledgeable – without education – about all the affairs of life and religion; both the useful and the harmful for the Muslim community.

The rest of their sects expanded the argument saying that knowledge is given to them and to other people, and they are not different from other people. Therefore, whoever receives knowledge from them – for life or religious affairs – can also receive the same knowledge from other people if he so chooses. If certain knowledge is not available from them or from other people, then it is permissi-

[1] ʿAbdullāh b. al-Ḥasan b. al-Ḥasan b. ʿAlī b. Abī Ṭālib (d. 145 AH) was called "al-Maḥḍ" (the pure), because his father and mother were the descendents of Imām ʿAlī and the Prophet. His father was al-Ḥasan's son and his mother was al-Ḥusayn's daughter. When his sons, Muḥammad and Ibrāhīm, revolted against al-Manṣūr, he was put in jail until he died.

ble for people to use their judgment (*ijtihād*) and to choose and to opine. This is the doctrine of the Zaydīyya – their strong and weak sects.

The Weak Zaydīyya

The weak Zaydīyya are called al-'Ijlīyya, who follow Hārūn b. Sa'īd al-'Ijlī.[1] And another sect of them was called al-Butrīyya, who follow Kathīr al-Nawwā', al-Ḥasan b. Ṣāliḥ b. Ḥay, Sālim b. Abī Ḥafṣa, al-Ḥakam b. 'Utayba, Salama b. Kuhayl, Abī al-Miqdām Thabit al-Ḥaddād. They asked the people to give their allegiance to 'Alī, peace be upon him, then they mixed this with the allegiance to Abū Bakr and 'Umar. This sect is considered, by non-Shī'a groups, the best sect because they prefer 'Alī *and* acknowledge the imāmate of Abū Bakr and 'Umar. They also criticize 'Uthmān, Talha, and al-Zubayr; and believe in fighting on the side of anyone from the sons of 'Alī, peace be upon him, as part of commanding the good and prohibiting the evil. They acknowledge the imāmate of any descendent of 'Alī when he revolts, but they do not designate an imām and wait until he revolts. According to them, all of 'Alī's descendents are equal, without regard to who their parents are.

[1] Hārūn b. Sa'īd al-'Ijlī (d. 145 AH) was one of the Zaydiyya chiefs. He was killed with Ibrāhīm b. 'Abdillāh b. al-Ḥasan, who revolted against al-Manṣūr.

The Strong Zaydīyya

The strong Zaydīyya are the followers of Abū al-Jārūd, the followers of Abū Khālid al-Wāsiṭī, and the followers of Fuḍayl al-Rassān and Manṣūr b. Abī al-Aswad.[1]

The Zaydīyya, who are called al-Ḥusaynīyya, say that whoever from the Family of Muḥammad calls to [the path of] Allāh, the Exalted, must be obeyed. They say that ʿAlī b. Abī Ṭālib was an imām when he called upon the people [to follow him] and declared his rule. After him, al-Ḥusayn was an imām when he revolted and before that too because he was not on good terms with Muʿāwiya and Yazīd b. Muʿāwiya until he was killed. Then was Zayd b. ʿAlī b. al-Ḥusayn, who was killed in Kūfa. His mother was a captive. Then his son, Yaḥyā b. Zayd b. ʿAlī,[2] who was killed in Khurāsān – his mother was Rayṭah bt. Abū Hāshim b. ʿAbdullāh b. Muḥammad b.

---

[1] Manṣūr b. Abī al-Aswad al-Laythī was praised by al-Najāshī (*Rijāl*, p. 353). He was also considered trustworthy by al-Dhahabi (*Mīzān* III, p. 200).

[2] Yaḥyā b. Zayd (d. 125 AH) participated in his father's uprising against the Umayyads. When his father was killed, he went to Balkh and began his own movement. He was killed during the caliphate of al-Walīd.

al-Ḥanafīyya. Then his other son, ʿĪsā b. Zayd b. ʿAlī,[1] whose mother was a captive too; and then Muḥammad b. ʿAbdullāh b. al-Ḥasan;[2] his mother was Hind bt. Abī ʿUbayda b. ʿAbdullāh b. Zamʿa b. al-Aswad b. al-Muṭṭalib b. Asad b. al-ʿUzzā b. Quṣay. After him anyone from the Family of Muḥammad, peace be upon him, and his family, who calls to the path of Allāh, is an imām.

The Mughīrīyya, followers of al-Mughīra b. Saʿīd, went along with [al-Ḥusaynīyya] until the imāmate of Muḥammad b. ʿAbdullāh b. al-Ḥasan, and associated themselves with him. When he was killed, they remained without an imām or an heir [of an imām]. They did not acknowledge the imāmate of anyone after him.

---

[1] ʿĪsā b. Zayd (d. 168 AH) was the other son of Zayd, who revolted against al-Manṣūr, with Muḥammad b. ʿAbdillāh and Ibrāhīm b. ʿAbdillāh. He was not killed in that uprising, but he elected to hide himself for the rest of his life.

[2] Muḥammad b. ʿAbdullāh b. al-Ḥasan b. al-Ḥasan b. ʿAlī b. Abī Ṭālib (d. 145 AH) was called "al-Nafs al-Zakiyya" (The Pure Soul). He and his brother, Ibrāhīm, revolted against al-Manṣūr. He managed to threaten the ʿAbbāsid regime and capture a huge territory (Medīna, Mecca, Baṣra, Fars, and Yemen). Al-Manṣūr sent an army of four thousand men and ended his threat.

Those Who Believed in the Imamate of al-Bāqir

As to those who acknowledged the imāmate of ʿAlī b. Abī Ṭālib, al-Ḥasan, al-Ḥusayn, and ʿAlī b. al-Ḥusayn, they went on to acknowledge the imāmate of Abū Jaʿfar Muḥammad b. ʿAlī b. al-Ḥusayn, al-Bāqir, peace be upon him. They remained on this belief until he died, except for a small circle that listened to a man named ʿAmr b. Riyāh, who claimed that he asked Abū Jaʿfar, peace be upon him, a question and received a certain answer. He claimed that he asked him the same question after a year and received a different answer. When he reminded him of the first answer, Abū Jaʿfar told him that the first answer might have been given while practicing the *taqīyyah*.[1]

---

[1] The doctrine of *taqiyyah* states that it is permissible for a person to hide certain beliefs or pretend to adhere to certain beliefs, in order to avoid any possible harm from the opponents. Although it is practiced by all Muslims, the doctrine became associated with the Shīʿa, who consider it one of their cardinal doctrines and practiced it more than their opponents, due to their permanent need for such practice to avoid oppression. The practice of *taqiyyah*, according to the Shīʿa, has three conditions. (1) It is mandatory, when sacrificing oneself would not change anything; (2) it is permissible, as long as it does not lead to corruption and oppression; (3) it is prohibited (*harām*), when it leads to corruption and oppression. One cannot kill an innocent person, to save oneself, and invoke the doctrine of *taqiyyah*.

He then had doubts about his imāmate. When he met with a follower of Abū Jaʿfar named Muḥammad b. Qays,[1] he told him, "I asked Abū Jaʿfar a question and he answered it; then I asked him the same question after a year and received a different answer. When I asked him why he did that, he claimed that he was practicing the *taqīyyah* (dissimulation). Allāh knows that I asked him for no reason other than my desire to learn and act according to his opinion, so he had no reason to practice the *taqīyyah* to avoid my harm." Muḥammad b. Qays said, "He might be afraid of another person." He said, "No other person was present in both occasions. Indeed, his two answers were contradictory because he did not memorize his first answer, so that he could repeat it the second time." He rescinded his belief in his imāmate and said, "The one who makes false rules under any circumstances, or rules against Allāh's commands practicing the *taqīyyah* closing his doors on himself is not an imām. An imām must revolt and command the good and prohibit the evil." He then accepted the belief of al-Butrīyya, along with a small circle of people, who followed him.

The rest of the followers of Abū Jaʿfar, peace be upon him, remained believing in his imāmate until his death in Dhul-Ḥijjah, 114 AH at the age of fifty-five years and several months. He was buried in Medīna, at the same burial place of his father, ʿAlī b. al-Ḥusayn, peace be upon him. He was born in the year 59 AH. Some say that he died in

---

[1] Muḥammad b. Qays al-Bajalī (d. 151 AH) was a follower of al-Bāqir and al-Ṣādiq. He wrote a book titled, *Qaḍāyā Amīr al-Mu'minīn Alayh as-Salām*. (Ṭusī, *Fihrist*, p. 161; Najāshī, *Rijāl*, 197-98)

the year 119 AH at the age of sixty-three years. His mother is Umm ʿAbdullāh bt. al-Ḥasan b. ʿAlī b. Abī Ṭālib. The duration of his imāmate was twenty-one years, and some say it was twenty-four years.

The Divergence After the Death of Al-Bāqir

The Mughīrīyya

When Abū Jaʿfar, peace be upon him, died, his followers became two sects. One sect believed in the imāmate of Muḥammad b. ʿAbdullāh b. al-Ḥasan b. al-Ḥasan b. ʿAlī b. Abī Ṭālib, who revolted in Medīna and was killed there. They claimed that he was al-Mahdī and that he was not killed, but is living in a mountain called "*al-ʿAlamīyyah*" on the road between Mecca and Najd, the large mountain to the left of the traveller to Mecca. He will remain there until his appearance, because the Messenger of Allāh, peace be upon him, and his family, said, "al-Mahdī is named after me and his father is named after my father." His brother, Ibrāhīm b. ʿAbdullāh b. al-Ḥasan, had revolted in Baṣra and asked the people to believe in the imāmate of his brother, Muḥammad b. ʿAbdullāh. When he became a threat, al-Manṣūr sent the army against him and he was killed after several battles. One of the people, who made this claim, was al-Mughīra b. Saʿīd, when Abū Jaʿfar Muḥammad b. ʿAlī died. When he announced this claim, the Shīʿa – followers of Abū ʿAbdullāh Jaʿfar b. Muḥammad, peace be upon them – shunned and rejected him. He then claimed that they were *Rāfiḍah*,[1] being the first to call them by this name. Some of the followers of al-Mughīra appointed him an imām and claimed that he was designated by al-Ḥusayn b. ʿAlī, then by ʿAlī b. al-Ḥusayn, then by Abū Jaʿfar Muḥammad b. ʿAlī, peace be upon them. They said that he was the imām, until al-Mahdī appears. They denied the imāmate of Abū ʿAbdullāh Jaʿfar b. Muḥammad, peace be upon him, – saying that there is no imāmate for the sons of ʿAlī b. Abī Ṭālib after Abū Jaʿfar Muḥammad b. ʿAlī, but the imāmate is reserved for al-Mughīra b. Saʿīd until the appearance of al-Mahdī. According to them, al-Mahdī is ʿAbdullāh b. al-Ḥasan b. al-Ḥasan, who is alive – he was not killed and he never died. This sect was called "the Mughīrīyya," after al-Mughīra b. Saʿīd, the servant of Khālid b. ʿAbdillāh al-Qasrī. Al-Mughīra went as far as

[1] The word *Rāfiḍah* is derived from "*rafḍ*" (rejection). There are several stories about the origin of this term and its reference to the Shīʿa, other than al-Nawbakhtī's story. Al-Ashʿarī said, "When [Zayd] revolted in Kūfa, with his followers, who gave him their allegiance, he heard some of them criticize Abū Bakr and ʿUmar. He objected to that. Therefore, the ones, who gave him allegiance left him. He said to them, 'You rejected me (*rafaḍtumūni.*)' They were called *Rāfiḍah*, because Zayd said to them, 'You rejected me' and remained with a small group." (*Maqālāt* I, p. 130) A similar story is narrated by Ibn al-Murtaḍā in *al-Munya wa al-Amal*, p. 93-4; and by al-Rāzī in the *Iʿtiqādāt*, p. 77. However, al-Baghdādi uses the term in reference to all sects of the Shīʿa, although he narrates the same story of al-Ashʿarī (*al-Farq bayn al-Firaq*, p. 21 & p. 35-6).

saying that he was a prophet and that Gabriel brings revelation from Allāh to him. Khālid b. ʿAbdillāh al-Qasrī arrested him and, when asked, he repeated his claims and refused to repent. Khālid killed and crucified him. He also claimed that he was able to revive the dead, in addition to his belief in metempsychosis. His followers believe in that until these days.

Those Who Believed in the Imamate of al-Sādiq

The second sect of the followers of Abū Jaʿfar Muḥammad b. ʿAlī, peace be upon him, believed in the imāmate of Abū ʿAbdullāh Jaʿfar b. Muḥammad, peace be upon him. They remained on this belief throughout his life, except for a few of them, who abandoned him after he hinted to the imāmate of his son, Ismāʿīl,[1] who died later during his life. They said, "He lied to us, thus he is not an imām, because the imāms do not lie, nor do they say that which is not going to occur." They claimed that Jaʿfar said that Allāh, the Exalted, changed His will (*badā lahū*) regarding the imāmate of Ismāʿīl. Therefore, they denied that the *badā*[2] and the will (*al-mashīʾah*) are

---

[1] Ismāʿīl b. Jaʿfar (d. 143 AH) is the ancestor of the Fāṭimid dynasty that ruled Egypt. He died during his father's life. Those who believe in his imāmate are called the Ismāʿīliyya.

[2] The doctrine of *badāʾ* is probably the most controversial issue in the debates between the Shīʿa and their opponents. In

possible from Allāh – saying that it was erroneous and impossible. They joined the Butrīyya, after that, and held the beliefs of Sulaymān b. Jarīr [al-Riqqī], who told his followers, after this incident, that the imāms of the *Rāfidah* made up two arguments for their *Shīʿa* to rule out any lying from their imāms: the *badā'* and the *taqīyyah*. As to the *badā'*, the imāms had placed themselves, for their Shīʿa, in the position of the prophets for their followers – concerning the knowledge of what was, what is, and what will be. They told their Shīʿa that certain events would occur in future (tomorrow). If is indeed happened, they would say to them, "Have we not told you about it before it occurred? We know from Allāh, the Exalted, what the prophets know, because there is between us and Allāh, the Exalted, the same means that conveyed knowledge to the prophets. If, however, what they foretold did not occur, they would say that Allāh had changed His will. The same goes for the *taqīyyah*. When the imāms were overwhelmed by the number of queries regarding permissions and prohibitions and other various religious

---

the polemics of the opponents, the Shīʿa appear to believe that Allah changes his mind about certain things, which is contradictory to the concept of His knowledge of what was, what is, and what will be. The Shīʿa explanation, however, is quite different. The doctrine states that Allah would reveal something about an event – that is not finally determined – to the angels and they tell the Prophets, who tell their followers. Then Allah changes the course of events to another direction that contradicts what the Prophet has said. (M. al-Kāshif al-Ghitā', *Asl al-Shīʿa wa Usūluhā*, p. 190; Al-Ashʿarī, *Maqālāt* I, p. 109)

sciences, they dictated their answers without remembering how they responded to each answer, because of the passing of time and variety of occasions in which they were asked. This caused the occurrence of contradictory answers to the same questions and similar answers to different questions. When people noticed this and asked them about the discrepancy in their answers and the reason for the difference in their responses, the imāms said, "When we answered in this way we were practicing the *taqīyyah*. We are allowed to do this, because we know what is good for you and what protects you and us from the enemies." How can anyone, then, catch them telling a lie, or tell their truth from their error? Hearing this argument, some of the followers of Abū Jaʿfar moved to the camp of Sulaymān b. Jarīr and abandoned their belief in the imāmate of Jaʿfar, peace be upon him.

The Divergence After the Death of Jaʿfar al-Ṣādiq

When Abū ʿAbdullāh Jaʿfar b. Muḥammad, peace be upon him, died – he died, peace be upon him, in Medīna in Shawwāl of 148 (AH) at the age of sixty-five. He was born in 83 (AH). He was buried in the same place of his father and grandfather in the *Baqīʿ* cemetery.[1] His imāmate was two months less than thirty-four years. His mother is Umm Farwah, daughter of al-Qāsim b. Muḥammad b. Abū Bakr, and her mother is Asmāʾ the daughter of ʿAbdurraḥmān b. Abū Bakr. His Shīʿa became six sects:

The Nāwūsīyya

One sect said that Jaʿfar b. Muḥammad did not die and that he will not die until he revolts and rules the people and that he is al-Mahdī. They quoted him as say-

[1] This is a well-known cemetery in Medīna. It is the burial place for many prominent Muslims. Among those is Fāṭima al-Zahrā', daughter of the Prophet, and the Imāms al-Ḥasan b. ʿAlī, ʿAlī b. al-Ḥusayn, Muḥammad al-Bāqir, and Jaʿfar al-Ṣādiq. When the Wahhābi forces came to power, they leveled these graves to the ground (following their doctrines about forbidding any building on gravesites).

ing, "If you see my head drop from a mountain, do not believe [in what you see], for I am your man." They also quoted him as saying, "If a man comes to you and says that he nursed me and washed my dead body and buried me, do not believe him, for I am your man – the owner of the Sword." This sect is called "the Nāwūsīyya." They had the name from their chief, a Baṣran named [ʿAjlān] b. Nāwūs.

The Ismāʿīlīyya

Another sect claimed that the imām after Jaʿfar b. Muḥammad was his son, Ismāʿīl b. Jaʿfar. They denied the death of Ismāʿīl during his father's life – saying that it was a trick plotted by his father, who was afraid for him, so he hid him. They claimed that Ismāʿīl would not die until he ruled the world and cared for the people, and that he was al-Mahdī, because his father appointed him for the imāmate after him and obligated them to accept that and told them that he [Ismāʿīl] was the man [after him]. They argued that the imām would not spread a lie. When the news of his death came to us, we believed [the imām] and that he is al-Mahdī and that he did not die. This sect is the pure Ismāʿīli sect. The mother of Ismāʿīl and his brother ʿAbdullāh, sons of Jaʿfar b. Muḥammad, peace be upon him, was Fāṭima, daughter of al-Ḥusayn b. al-Ḥasan b. ʿAlī b. Abī Ṭālib, peace be upon him. Her mother was Asmāʾ, daughter of ʿAqīl b. Abī Ṭālib, peace be upon them.

The Mubārakīyya

A third sect said that the imām after Jaʿfar b. Muḥammad was Muḥammad b. Ismāʿīl b. Jaʿfar.[1] His mother was a captive woman. They said that Ismāʿīl was the imām during his father's life, and when he died before his father it was rightfully transferred to Muḥammad b. Ismāʿīl – and any other claim would be wrong – because the imāmate does not go among brothers after al-Ḥasan and al-Ḥusayn, peace be upon them. It can only go to [the imam's] progeny. Therefore, ʿAbdullāh and Mūsā, brothers of Ismāʿīl did not have any right to it, just like Muḥammad b. al-Ḥanafīyya did not have any right to compete with ʿAlī b. al-Ḥusayn. This sect is called "the Mubārakīyya" after their chief, al-Mubārak, who was a servant of Ismāʿīl b. Jaʿfar.

The Khaṭṭābīyya

The Ismāʿīlīyya are the Khaṭṭābīyya, followers of Abū al-Khaṭṭāb Muḥammad b. Abī Zaynab al-Asadī al-Ajdaʿ. One of their sects joined the sect of Muḥammad b. Ismāʿīl and acknowledged the death of Ismāʿīl b. Jaʿfar during his father's life. These are the ones, who revolted

---

[1] Muḥammad b. Ismāʿīl al-Maktūm (d. *ca.* 198 AH) was considered the first of the hidden imāms, according to the Ismāʿīliyya. Al-Kashshī narrates a story about him that he went to Baghdād and told Hārūn al-Rashīd that Imām Mūsā b. Jaʿfar is acting like a second caliph. (*Rijāl*, pp. 263-65)

during the life of Abū ʿAbdullāh Jaʿfar b. Muḥammad, peace be upon him, and fought against ʿĪsā b. Mūsā b. Muḥammad b. ʿAbdullāh b. al-ʿAbbās, who was the governor of Kūfa. When he heard that they permitted irreligious acts and claimed the prophethood of Abū al-Khaṭṭāb, he sent his force to the Mosque of Kūfa, where they gathered. They resisted him, so he had to kill them all. They were seventy men. Only one of them survived. He was wounded and the soldiers believed that they had already killed him. His name was Abū Salama, Sālim b. Mukarram al-Jammāl – also known as Abū Khadījah.[1] He claimed that he died and returned to life. They fought fiercely against ʿĪsā, using rocks and reeds instead of lances, because Abū al-Khaṭṭāb told them, "Fight them, for your reeds will hurt them like lances and swords, whereas their lances and swords will not harm you." He sent them to fight into groups of ten men each. When thirty of them were killed, they asked him, "Don't you see what they are doing to us, while our reeds do not harm them at all?" It was said that he told them, "What can I do? It seems that Allāh has changed his mind about you (*badā li-llāhi fīkum*). The Shīʿa narrated that he told his associates, "You were tested and your death was permitted. So fight in defense of your religion and reputation. Do not surrender your town and accept humiliation, since you will not escape being killed anyway. So die in dignity." They fought until the last one of them was killed. Abū al-Khaṭṭāb was captured and brought to ʿĪsā b. Mūsā, who killed him in Dār ar-Rizq – near the bank

[1] The story of Sālim b. Mukarram is narrated by al-Kashshī, who said that he repented after his survival. (*Rijāl*, pp. 352-53)

of the Euphrates – and crucified him with some of his associates and burned them later. He sent their heads to al-Manṣūr, who crucified them at the gate of Baghdād for three days before they were burned. Some of his followers said, "Abū al-Khaṭṭāb and his associates were not killed, but their enemies were confused and killed others, who resembled them, because they fought according to the orders of Abū ʿAbdullāh Jaʿfar b. Muḥammad. They left the Mosque without being seen or wounded. Indeed, their enemies were killing each other, thinking that they were killing the associates of Abū al-Khaṭṭāb, until the night fell. In the morning they examined the dead and discovered that all of them were their partners. They did not find any of the associates of Abū al-Khaṭṭāb among the dead or the wounded." This sect is the one claiming that Abū al-Khaṭṭāb was a prophet sent by Jaʿfar b. Muḥammad, then he made him one of the angels after this incident – may Allāh curse whomever makes such claim. After his death, his followers from Kūfa and other places joined Muḥammad b. Ismāʿīl b. Jaʿfar and acknowledged his imāmate and did not deviate [from this belief].

The sects of the *ghulāt* were divided after him with many doctrines. They also disagreed about their leaders and beliefs. One sect said that the spirit of Jaʿfar b. Muḥammad went to Abū al-Khaṭṭāb and moved, after the disappearance of Abū al-Khaṭṭāb, to Muḥammad b. Ismāʿīl b. Jaʿfar. Then they claimed the imāmate for the sons of Muḥammad b. Ismāʿīl.

The Qarāmiṭa

Another sect emerged from the Mubārakīyya, who shared this doctrine. They were called the Qarāmiṭa, after one of their chiefs, a man from the Land of *Sawād*[1] named Qurmuṭawayh.[2] They were originally from the Mubārakīyya sect before they deviated from them and said, "There are only seven imāms after the Prophet, peace be upon him, and his family. These are ʿAlī b. Abī Ṭālib (who is an imām-prophet), al-Ḥasan, al-Ḥusayn, ʿAlī b. al-Ḥusayn, Muḥammad b. ʿAlī [al-Bāqir], Jaʿfar b. Muḥammad, and Muḥammad b. Ismāʿīl b. Jaʿfar, who is al-Qā'im al-Mahdī and he is a prophet." They claimed that the prophethood was discontinued from the Prophet, peace be upon him, and his family, on the day that he was ordered to designate ʿAlī b. Abī Ṭālib, peace be upon him, at *Ghadīr Khum*. They also claimed that, on that day, the Prophethood went to ʿAlī b. Abī Ṭālib. They cited the statement of the Messenger of Allāh, peace be upon him, and his family, "Whoever had me for a master must now have ʿAlī as his master." This statement meant the transfer of the Prophethood and the Message to ʿAlī b. Abī Ṭālib, in compliance with the command of Allāh, the Exalted, and the Prophet, peace be upon him, and his fam-

[1] Iraq and Ahwāz used to be called by this name, because of its trees and cultivation, it appears black to the traveler from the south.

[2] He is called Ḥamdān Qurmuṭ or Qarmaṭ, because of the way he walked.

ily, became a follower of ʿAlī and obligated to him, from that day on. When ʿAlī, peace be upon him, died, the imāmate went to al-Ḥasan, then it went to al-Ḥusayn, then it went to ʿAlī b. al-Ḥusayn, then it went to Muḥammad b. ʿAlī, then it went to Jaʿfar b. Muḥammad. The imāmate was discontinued from Jaʿfar, during his life, and went to Ismāʿīl b. Jaʿfar, like it was discontinued from Muḥammad, peace be upon him, and his family, during his life. Then Allāh, the Exalted changed his mind (*badā lahū*) about the imāmate of Jaʿfar and Ismāʿīl and transferred it to Muḥammad b. Ismāʿīl. They cited a statement, which they attributed to Jaʿfar b. Muḥammad, peace be upon them, that he said, "I have not seen like the *badā'* of Allāh, the Exalted, about Ismāʿīl." They claimed that Muḥammad b. Ismāʿīl did not die and that he is in the land of the Romans, saying that he is al-Qā'im al-Mahdī. The meaning of al-Qā'im, according to them, is that he will be sent with a new "message" and a new divine law, which abrogates the law of Muḥammad, peace be upon him, and his family. They claimed that Muḥammad b. Ismāʿīl is one of the Cardinal Prophets (*ulū al-ʿazm*).[1] They count seven Prophets as *ulū al-ʿazm*: Nūḥ (Noah), Ibrāhīm (Abraham), Mūsā (Moses), ʿĪsā (Jesus), Muḥammad (peace be upon him and his family and all of them), ʿAlī, peace be upon him, and Muḥammad b. Ismāʿīl. They based his doctrine on the idea that the Heavens are seven, the levels of the earth are seven, and

[1] The reference to these prophets is taken from the Qur'ān (46:35). The verse, however, does not specify these prophets by their names.

man, too, has seven body-parts: two hands, two legs, a dorsum, an abdomen, and a heart. Man's head also has seven parts: two eyes, two ears, two nostrils, a mouth, which contains the tongue in the same way the heart is contained by the chest. The imāms are like that; their heart is Muḥammad b. Ismāʿīl. Regarding the abrogation of the law of Muḥammad, peace be upon him, and his family, they cited statements attributed to Abū ʿAbdullāh Jaʿfar b. Muḥammad, peace be upon him, claiming that he said, "When our Qāʾim rises, you will know the Qurʾān anew." They also claimed that he had said, "Islām started as a stranger and will be a stranger again – blessed are the strangers." They said that Allāh, the Exalted, gave the paradise of Adam, peace be upon him, to Muḥammad b. Ismāʿīl. This means to them permitting all irreligious acts and everything that exists in this life, as the statement of Allāh, the Exalted, indicates: "Eat of the bountiful things therein as you [two] please, but do not approach this tree." (Qurʾān, 2:35) ([The tree] means Mūsā b. Jaʿfar b. Muḥammad and his sons, who claimed the imāmate after him). [This sect] also claimed that Muḥammad b. Ismāʿīl was the seal of the prophets, who was mentioned by Allāh, the Exalted, in His Book. They also claimed that the world is made of twelve islands, each one has a witness (*ḥujja*) and each one of the twelve witnesses has a delegate (*dāʿiya*) and each delegate has a helping hand (*yad*), who is a man armed with proofs and signs in his favor. They call the witness a "father," the delegate a "mother," and the helping hand a "son," in the same way the believers in the Trinity argue that Allāh is one of three and He is the "Father" – He is certainly above that – and the Messiah, peace be upon him, is the "Son" and his mother is Maryam, peace be upon her.

They claimed that the Grand Witness is God and that he is the father; and the delegate is the mother; and the helping hand is the son – there is no doubt that those polytheists are liars, misguided, and losers. They claimed that all things mandated by Allāh, the Exalted, for his servants, which were emphasized by His Messenger, peace be upon him, and his family, have esoteric and exterior meanings. All the exterior meanings of the religious laws, which Allāh made obligatory (in the Qurʾān and the *sunnah*), are analogies underscored by esoteric meanings, which are the means for salvation. The exterior meanings, on the other hand, cause their followers torment and destruction. They are part of temporal punishment and torment for those who apply them. Allāh punished them because they did not know the truth and did not believe in it. This is the doctrine of the majority of Abū al-Khaṭṭāb's followers. They permitted the killing of people by swords, like the Bayhasīyya[1] and the Azāriqa[2] – from the Khawārij – allowed the killing of [Muslims] and the confiscation of their property and calling them unbelievers. They cited the statement of Allāh, the Exalted, "Slay

[1] The Bayhasiyya are the followers of Abū Bayhas, al-Hayṣam b. Jābir. They are one of the Khawārij sects. They believed that their opponents are unbelievers, like the opponents of the Prophet. See the description of their doctrines in *al-Milal wa al-Niḥal*, pp. 121-24.

[2] The Azāriqa are the followers of Nāfiʿ b. al-Azraq (d. 65 A.H). They managed to pose a threat for the Umayyads for over nineteen years. They believed in killing their opponents and their women and children. (*Milal*, pp. 111-16)

the unbelievers wherever you find them." (Qurʾān, 9:5) They also permitted taking their wives as captives and killing their children, citing the statement of Allāh, the Exalted, "Do not leave of the unbelievers a single one on earth." (Qurʾān, 71:26) They claimed that they had to begin by killing those who held different doctrines about the imāmate than their own doctrine, especially the believers in the imāmate of Mūsā b. Jaʿfar and his sons after him. They cited, for this priority, the statement of Allāh, the Exalted, "Fight those unbelievers who are near to you and let them find harshness in you." (Qurʾān, 9:23) They said, "Our first priority is to start with these adversaries, then the rest of the people." The number of this sect is large, but they have no clout or power. Most of them are in the vicinity of Kūfa and in Yemen, where their real count might reach approximately hundred thousand.

The Sumayṭīyya

The fourth sect of Abū ʿAbdullāh Jaʿfar b. Muḥammad's followers said that the imām after Jaʿfar was his son, Muḥammad b. Jaʿfar,[1] whose mother was a captive woman called Ḥamīda. He, Mūsā, and Isḥāq had the same mother. Some of them told a story that Muḥammad b. Jaʿfar entered his father's room, one day during his

[1] Muḥammad b. Jaʿfar Ad-Dībāj (d. 203 AH) revolted against al-Maʾmūn in 199 AH and managed to control the Ḥijāz territories. He was finally defeated and received an amnesty to surrender. He reconciled with al-Maʾmūn and remained close to him until he died.

childhood, and ran toward his father and stumbled with his gown. When he fell on his face, his father stood up, kissed him, removed the sand from his face, and took him to his chest. He said, "I heard my father saying: 'When you have a son, who resembles me, name him after me. For he resembles me and resembles the Messenger of Allāh, peace be upon him, and his family, and he follows his *Sunna*.'" Therefore, this sect claimed the imāmate for Muḥammad b. Jaʿfar and his sons after him. This sect is called the Sumayṭīyya, after one of their chiefs whose name was Yaḥyā b. Abī al-Sumayṭ.[1]

The Faṭḥīyya

The fifth sect said that the imāmate after Jaʿfar went to his son, ʿAbdullāh b. Jaʿfar al-Afṭaḥ,[2] because he was his father's the oldest son. He sat in his father's place and claimed the imāmate for himself. They cited a statement they attributed to Abū ʿAbdullāh Jaʿfar b. Muḥammad that "the imāmate belongs to the oldest of the imām's sons." Most of the believers in his father's imāmate ac-

[1] His name was also reported as "Yaḥyā b. Shumayṭ" (*al-Farq bayn al-Firaq*, p. 61; *Milal*, p. 168)

[2] ʿAbdullāh b. Jaʿfar al-Afṭaḥ (d. 148 AH) was the oldest son of Jaʿfar al-Ṣādiq. He was called "al-Afṭaḥ" because his head had a flat appearance, and some people say his feet were flat. He claimed the imāmate after his father, but died soon thereafter, without leaving any progeny. (al-Kashshī, *Rijāl*, p. 254-55)

knowledged the imāmate of ʿAbdullāh. Only a few people knew the truth and asked ʿAbdullāh some questions about what is permitted and what is not in the matters pertaining to prayer and alms. They did not find any knowledge in him. This sect, which claims the imāmate for ʿAbdullāh b. Jaʿfar, is the Faṭḥīyyah. They acquired this name because ʿAbdullāh had a flat head (*afṭaḥ*) – or flat feet, according to other accounts. Other people said that this sect was named after one of their chiefs, a Kūfan named ʿAbdullāh b. Fuṭayḥ. This sect attracted most Shīʿite notables and jurists, who had no doubt that ʿAbdullāh b. Jaʿfar deserved the imāmate, and that it belonged to his sons after him. But ʿAbdullāh died without leaving a son. Therefore, the vast majority of the Faṭḥīyyah returned to acknowledging the imāmate of Mūsā b. Jaʿfar[1]. Some of them returned to Mūsā b. Jaʿfar, peace be upon them, during the life of ʿAbdullāh, while their majority returned after his death, except for a few of them, who continued to believe in his imāmate and the imāmate of Mūsā b. Jaʿfar after him. ʿAbdullāh lived about seventy days after his father.

The sixth sect said that Mūsā b. Jaʿfar is the imām after his father. They denied the imāmate of ʿAbdullāh and said that he took the wrong action by siting in his father's place and claiming the imāmate. Among these were nota-

---

[1] Mūsā b. Jaʿfar, also named "al-Kāẓim" (d. 183 AH) is the seventh Imām for the Twelver Shīʿa. Hārūn al-Rashīd felt that he might threaten the ʿAbbāsid rule, so he took him to Baṣra and left him in prison for a year. Then he was brought to another prison in Baghdād, where he remained until he died. It is said that he was poisoned in prison.

ble associates of Abū ʿAbdullāh, peace be upon him, like Hishām b. Sālim[1], ʿAbdullāh b. Yaʿfūr[2], ʿUmar b. Yazīd (the silk merchant)[3], Muḥammad b. al-Nuʿmān Abū Jaʿfar al-Aḥwal (*Mu'min al-Ṭāq*)[4], ʿUbayd b. Zurāra[5], Jamīl b. Darrāj[6], Ibān b. Taghlib[7], and Hishām b. al-Ḥakam[1] –

---

[1] Hishām b. Sālim al-Jawālīqī was a follower of al-Ṣādiq and al-Kāẓim. Al-Kashshī narrated many stories about him; some were in his favor, while others were against him. (Ṭūsī, *Fihrist*, 207; Kashshī, *Rijāl*, pp. 281-85)

[2] ʿAbdullāh b. Abī Yaʿfūr was a trusted companion of Imām Jaʿfar al-Ṣādiq. Al-Kashshī quoted Jaʿfar al-Ṣādiq as saying, "I have not found anyone, who takes my advice and obeys my orders except for ʿAbdullāh b. Abī Yaʿfūr. (*Rijāl*, p. 246)

[3] ʿUmar b. Yazīd was a close companion of Imām al-Ṣādiq. He said that al-Ṣādiq told him, "Son of Yazīd! By Allah, You are one of us, the family of the Prophet." (al-Kashshī, *Rijāl*, p. 331)

[4] The opponents of Shīʿism call him *Shayṭān al-Ṭāq*. He was sharp in his answers. (al-Kashshī, *Rijāl*, p. 185-91) He wrote many books in defense of the doctrines of Shīʿism. (Ṭūsī, *Fihrist*, pp. 161-2)

[5] ʿUbayd b. Zurāra b. Aʿyun (d. 150 AH) was one of the students of al-Ṣādiq. (Ṭūsī, *Fihrist*, pp. 137-8)

[6] He was highly praised by al-Ṭūsī and al-Kashshī. (Ṭūsī, *Fihrist*, p. 73)

[7] He was a close companion of al-Ṣādiq, who ordered him to sit in the mosque and answer people's questions. Al-Ṭūsī reports his death in 141 AH – during the life of Imām Jaʿfar al-

among many other notables of the Shīʿa and their scholars and jurists. They all insisted on the imāmate of Mūsā b. Jaʿfar until most of the believers in the imāmate of ʿAbdullāh b. Jaʿfar converted to their side and acknowledged the imāmate of Mūsā b. Jaʿfar. However, a small circle kept the belief in the imāmate of ʿAbdullāh b. Jaʿfar and acknowledged Mūsā after him, permitting the imāmate of two brothers, after their previous opposition to [the imāmate of two brothers.]. Among these are ʿAbdullāh b. Bukayr b. Aʿyan[2], ʿAmmār b. Mūsā Al-Sābāṭī[3], and few others, who followed them. As for the followers of Mūsā b. Jaʿfar, they did not disagree about him. They continued in their belief until his second imprisonment. They had doubts about his imāmate when he was imprisoned a second time, during which he died in al-Rashīd's jail. They then became five sects.

Ṣādiq. In this case, he could not be mentioned among these men. (Ṭūsī, *Fihrist*, pp. 44-46)

[1] Hishām b. al-Ḥakam (d. 199 AH) was the head of the Shīʿa of his time. The opponents of the Shīʿa attribute many doctrines to him that are inconsistent with Shīʿism. He wrote many books in defense of Shīʿism. (Ṭūsī, *Fihrist*, pp. 207-9)

[2] Al-Ṭūsī considered him trustworthy despite his being one of the Faṭḥiyyah. (Ṭūsī, *Fihrist*, p. 136)

[3] He was praised by al-Kashshī, al-Mufīd, and al-Ṭūsī, who mentioned "a large good and trustworthy book," which he wrote. It is probably a *Ḥadīth* book. (Fihrist, p. 147-8)

The Qaṭʿīyya

One sect said that he [Mūsā b. Jaʿfar] died in the jail of al-Sindī b. Shāhak[1] and that Yaḥyā b. Khālid[2] fed him poisoned dates and grape and caused his death. They said that the imām after Mūsā is ʿAlī b. Mūsā al-Riḍā.[3] This sect was called the Qaṭʿīyya, because they affirmed (*qaṭaʿū*) that Mūsā b. Jaʿfar had died and that ʿAlī, his son, was the imām after him. They did not waver about their position, nor did they have any doubts. Indeed, they followed the original path.

---

[1] He was the head of al-Rashīd's guards. It is said that he poisoned Imām Mūsā al-Kāẓim, who was in his prison.

[2] Yaḥyā b. Khālid al-Barmakī (d. 190 A.H) was the teacher of Hārūn al-Rashīd. He acquired tremendous power during the caliphate of al-Rashīd, who appointed him for the head minister position. He then sent him to prison for the rest of his life.

[3] ʿAlī b. Mūsā al-Riḍā (d. 203 AH) was the eighth Imām of the Twelver Shīʿa. Al-Maʾmūn appointed him for the caliphate after himself and ordered that some of the currency be coined with his name on it. al-Riḍā agreed to the arrangement on the condition that he does not participate in the decision making process. This event excited the wrath of the ʿAbbāsids against al-Maʾmūn. He had to fight their rebellion in Iraq, where they appointed an other caliph to substitute him. Al-Ridā died before al-Maʾmūn and was buried in Ṭūs, northeastern Iran.

Another sect said that Mūsā b. Jaʿfar did not die, nor will he die until he rules the world from east to west. He would fill it with justice after it had been filled with oppression. They claimed that he was al-Qāʾim al-Mahdī. They also asserted that "he escaped from jail in broad daylight without being seen or felt by anyone. The rulers and his followers then claimed that he died to confuse the people. Indeed, he disappeared and remained in hiding." They also attributed many statements to his father, Jaʿfar b. Muḥammad, peace be upon them, saying that he was al-Qāʾim al-Mahdī; if his head is thrown down the side of a mountain and you see it descending onto you, do not believe [that he died], for he *is* al-Qāʾim.

Others said that he died and that the imāmate would not go to anyone until he returned and victoriously uprose. They claimed that he did return after his death and that he is hiding in an unrevealed location, giving orders to his close followers, who see him and meet with him. They cited certain statements made by his father that al-Qāʾim acquired this name because he rises (*yaqūmu*) after his death.

Others said that he died and that he is al-Qāʾim, who resembles ʿĪsā (Jesus) b. Maryam, peace be upon him. They said that he had not yet returned, but that he would return at a determined time to fill the world with justice after it had been filled with oppression. They said that his father stated that he resembles ʿĪsā b. Maryam and he will be killed by the hands of the descendents of al-ʿAbbās, as it really happened.

The Wāqifa (The Mamṭūra)

Some of them denied that he was killed. They said that he had died and that Allāh had lifted him up to His domain and that He would send him back when he rose. All of these were called the Wāqifa[1] (the Halting Sect), because they stopped at Mūsā b. Jaʿfar – as the imām al-Qā'im. They did not follow an imām after him, nor did they pass him and follow another. Those of them who claimed that he was alive, said that al-Riḍā, peace be upon him, and his successors were not imāms; rather, they were [Mūsā's] deputies – one after another – until the time of his return, and that people have to obey them and follow their orders. The Wāqifa were called "*the Mamṭūra*" by their opponents, who supported ʿAlī b. Mūsā. This name prevailed and became widespread. The origin of this [name] was that ʿAlī b. Ismāʿīl al-Maythamī and Yūnus b. ʿAbdurraḥmān had a heated debate, at the end of which ʿAlī b. Ismāʿīl told his adversary, "You are nothing but rain-soaked dogs (*kilāb mamṭūra*)," meaning that they

---

[1] This doctrine started with two deputies of Mūsā b. Jaʿfar, who received thirty thousand Dinārs from the family of Banū al-Ashʿath, in fulfilment of their alms duty. One of these men was called Ḥayyān al-Sarrāj. The Imām was in prison at the time, so these two men used the money to buy houses and other types of property. When they heard that the Imām died, they denied his death and spread the doctrine among the Shīʿa that he does not die, because he is al-Qā'im. Many people believed their statement. They did that out of greed. (Al-Kashshī, *Rijāl*, pp. 459-60)

stink more than rotten carcasses, because dogs, after being soaked by rain, smell worse than rotten carcasses. This epithet stuck to them [until] now; because, if one is told, "You are *mamṭūr*," it becomes clear that he is one of those who stopped at Mūsā b. Jaʿfar in particular. Since after every other [imām] there was a sect that stopped at him, this epithet is specific to the *wāqifa* of Mūsā.

Another sect said, "We do not know whether he is dead or alive, because we have narrated many stories about his being al-Qāʾim al-Mahdī. It is not permissible to retract them. We have also received true accounts about the death of his father, his grandfather, and his other ancestors, peace be upon them. This is also something that we cannot dispute, because of its publicity and authenticity, so that it cannot be considered some sort of conspiracy – for death is our just fate and Allāh, the Exalted, does whatever he wills. Therefore, we stopped and hesitated to choose between confirming his death or his being alive. Meanwhile, we continue to adhere to his imāmate. We will not move to another [imām] until we become certain about his affair and the veracity of this self-appointed man, who claimed the imāmate," meaning ʿAlī b. Mūsā al-Riḍā. "If his imāmate becomes authenticated, like his father's imāmate, through essential signs and proofs that he is the imām and that his father has died, and not through the stories of his associates, we will believe him and give him our loyalty. This sect is also part of the Mamṭūra. Some of them saw certain proofs from Abū al-Ḥasan al-Riḍā and believed in his imāmate. A group of them also believed the accounts of his associates and their opinions about him and converted to acknowledging his imāmate.

The Bishrīyya

Another sect called the Bishrīyya, followers of Muḥammad b. Bashīr[1], a Kūfan client (*mawlā*) of Banū Asad. They said that Mūsā b. Jaʿfar did not die or enter any jail, and that he was alive, but that he did not appear. They said that he was al-Qāʾim al-Mahdī and that, before going undercover, he had designated Muḥammad b. Bashīr as his heir and given him his seal and taught him everything his followers would need. He fully authorized him and placed him in his position. Therefore, Muḥammad b. Bashīr was the imām after him. Before Muḥammad b. Bashīr died, he designated his own son, Samīʿ b. Muḥammad b. Bashīr, as the imām. The next imām should be the one designated by Samīʿ, and will be the imām that must be obeyed by the whole community until the appearance of Mūsā. Anything that is mandatory to be paid, as religious duty or alms, must be paid to these [men] until the rise of al-Qāʾim. They claimed that ʿAlī b. Mūsā and the rest of Mūsā's descendents, who claimed the imāmate were not legitimately born. They disputed their lineage and accused them of blasphemy for claiming the imāmate. They also called anyone who believed in their imāmate blasphemers and permitted shedding their blood and confiscating their property. They also re-

---

[1] He lived during the time of Imām Mūsā b. Jaʿfar and his son, Imām al-Riḍā. Both of them cursed him and wished for him the worst type of death, which he faced. (Al-Kashshī, *Rijāl*, pp. 477-83)

stricted the religious duties to the five prayers, and fasting, denying the obligation of alms, Hajj, and the rest of religious duties. Further, they permitted forbidden sexuality: incest and homosexuality. They cited the statement of Allāh, the Exalted, "Or He couples them, males and females." (Qurʾān, 42:50) They believed in metempsychosis, saying that the imāms are one person, who moves from one body to another. They also made it incumbent upon themselves to distribute their wealth and all their belongings, and anything that is allocated [to be spent] for the sake of Allāh should be delivered to Samīʿ and his deputies after him. Their doctrines on free will (*tafwīḍ*) are the same doctrines of free-will extremists.

Mūsā b. Jaʿfar, peace be upon him, was born in 128 AH – or, according to some, in 129 AH; al-Rashīd moved him from Medīna ten nights before the end of Shawwāl 179 AH; al-Rashīd came to visit Mecca for the *ʿumra* of Ramaḍān and then went for the *Ḥajj*; and took [Mūsā b. Jaʿfar] with him to Baṣra, wherein he placed him in the jail of ʿĪsā b. Jaʿfar b. Abī Jaʿfar al-Manṣūr. Then he summoned him to Baghdād and placed him in the jail of al-Sindī b. Shāhak. He died in jail, in Baghdad, five nights before the end of Rajab 183 AH. He was fifty-five years old – or fifty-four – and was buried in the cemetery of Quraysh. According to another account, he was buried with his chains on, in fulfilment of his own will. The duration of his imāmate was thirty-five years and a few months. His mother was a captive named Ḥamīda, who is also the mother of his two brothers Isḥāq and Muḥammad – the sons of Jaʿfar b. Muḥammad, peace be upon him.

The Divergence After the Death of al-Riḍā

The followers of ʿAlī b. Mūsā al-Riḍā were divided after his death and became several sects. One sect said that, after ʿAlī b. Mūsā, peace be upon him, the imāmate belonged to his son, Muḥammad b. ʿAlī,[1] peace be upon him, who married the daughter of al-Ma'mūn. He [i.e. ʿAlī b. Mūsā] had no other son. They followed the customary will, as it was formed by the Prophet, peace be upon him, and his family.

Another sect believed in the imāmate of Aḥmad b. Mūsā b. Jaʿfar.[2] They said that his father designated him and al-Riḍā, peace be upon him. They accepted the imāmate of two brothers, saying that his father designated him an heir after ʿAlī b. Mūsā, which is similar to the claim of the Faṭḥīyya.

---

[1] Muḥammad al-Jawād (d. 220 AH) is the ninth Imām of the Twelver Shīʿa. He was very young when his father died. He married the daughter of al-Ma'mūn.

[2] Aḥmad b. Mūsā b. Jaʿfar was a pious man. He was killed during a battle between him and the governor of Shīrāz, who prevented him from going to Khurāsān. His shrine is still in Shīrāz and is called "Shāh-i Chirāgh."

The Mu'allifa

Another sect named the Mu'allifa of the Shīʿa. They supported the right position and acknowledged the imāmate of ʿAlī b. Mūsā [al-Riḍā], after confirming the death of his father. They were right up to that point; however, when al-Riḍā, peace be upon him, died, they returned to believe in the termination of the imāmate after Mūsā b. Jaʿfar, peace be upon him.

The Muḥadditha

Another sect was named the Muḥadditha, who were part of the Murjiʿa and the people of Ḥadīth. They entered among those who acknowledged the imāmate of Mūsā b. Jaʿfar and the imāmate of ʿAlī b. Mūsā, becoming Shīʿa for the sake of worldly goods. When ʿAlī b. Mūsā, peace be upon him, died, they returned to their original belief.

Another sect was part of the strong Zaydīyya. They acknowledged the imāmate of ʿAlī b. Mūsā, peace be upon him, when al-Ma'mūn designated him as his heir for the caliphate. They too were seeking worldly goods, managing to deceive the people for a while. When ʿAlī b. Mūsā, peace be upon him, died, they returned to their original belief and joined their fellow Zaydīyya.

ʿAlī b. Mūsā, peace be upon him, died in Ṭūs, a small town in Khurāsān. He was travelling to Iraq with al-Ma'mūn at the end of Ṣafar in 203 AH. He was fifty-five years old. His birth was in 151 AH – or 153 AH, according to some people – and the duration of his imāmate was twenty years and seven months. He was buried in Ṭūs, in the house of Ḥamīd b. Quḥṭuba al-Ṭāʾī.[1] His mother was a captive woman named Shahd – and some said that her name was Najīyya. He was the oldest son of Mūsā b. Jaʿfar. His siblings are thirty-two – seventeen brothers and fifteen sisters – from captive women. ʿAlī b. Mūsā, peace be upon him, joined al-Maʾmūn, accompanied by Rajaʾ b. Abī al-Ḍaḥḥāk[2] at the end of 200 AH. He took the road of Baṣra and Fārs. Al-Riḍā, peace be upon him, married al-Maʾmūn's daughter.

---

[1] Ḥamīd b. Quḥṭuba al-Ṭāʾī (d. 159 AH) was a famous ʿAbbāsid general. He was the governor of Khurāsān during the last years of his life.

[2] He was the land-tax officer for al-Maʾmūn. Then, he occupied similar positions for the next two ʿAbbāsid caliphs, al-Muʿtaṣim and al-Wāthiq. He was killed by the governor of Damascus in 226 AH.

The Divergence About the Imamate of Muḥammad b. ʿAlī

The reason that one sect believed in the imāmate of Aḥmad b. Mūsā, and another sect believed in the termination of the imāmate, was that Abū al-Ḥasan al-Riḍā, peace be upon him, died when his son was seven years old. They considered him a child, saying, "The imām must be a mature adult. If Allāh, the Exalted, were to mandate the obedience of non-adults, it would be possible that He burdens non-adults [with religious duties]. As it is incomprehensible that non-adults would carry the religious burden, a non-adult cannot understand the judgment among people. He would not comprehend the intricacies of jurisprudence and divine law, in addition to all of the teaching of the Prophet, peace be upon him, and his family, which is needed by the people for their religion and life until the Day of Judgment. If it were possible for a child, who is one step before adulthood, to understand all this, it would be possible for those who are two, three, or four steps away from that. Then it would be possible for those in early childhood and the infants in their cradles, which is incomprehensible, irrational, and uncommon.

The ones, who believed in the imāmate of Abū Jaʿfar Muḥammad b. ʿAlī b. Mūsā, peace be upon them, disagreed about the source of his knowledge, because of his young age. They asked one another: "The imām must be knowledgeable. Since Abū Jaʿfar is not an adult and his father has died, how did he become knowledgeable, and where did his knowledge come from?"

Some said that his knowledge could not come from his father, who was carried to Khurāsān when the age of Abū Jaʿfar was four years and several months. A person of this age, is not able to attain the knowledge of intricate and grand religious matters. Indeed, Allāh, the Exalted, taught him all of that when he reached adulthood, by the means of knowledge, which are available for the imāms – such as inspiration, echoing in the ears, true dreams, a counseling angel [and other means], as it was indicated in the authentic and indisputable reports (*akhbār*) that came to us through reliable chains of transmission.

Some of them said, before his adulthood, "He is the imām in the sense that the imāmate belongs to him particularly, and not to another, until he reaches adulthood. When he reaches that age, he becomes knowledgeable, not through inspiration or a counseling angel or anything like that," which was claimed by the previous sect, "because the revelation stopped after the death of the Prophet, peace be upon him, according to the consensus of [Muslim] community. Also, inspiration is something that arrives to you when you contemplate. It is the knowledge about something, which you have already experienced. This is not something by which religious laws, numerous as they are, can be known. Since they have different causes and different fundamental principles, one has to obtain their knowledge through hearing [i.e. learning from others]. If a person has the soundest mind and best contemplative faculty and he never heard that one has to prostrate four times at the Noon Prayer, three times at Sunset Prayer, and twice at dawn prayer, he would not be able to deduct this information by depending on his mind or contemplative faculty alone. He also would not arrive at this [knowledge] by chance or the help of his lucky stars. It is incomprehensible that such knowledge would be attained without education. Therefore, it is invalid to claim that he attained his knowledge through luck and inspiration. Instead, we say that he attained his knowledge, after becoming a mature adult, from his father's books, whose knowledge he has inherited. In them, all major and minor sciences were explained." Some members of this sect say that the imām is permitted to use analogy (*qiyās*) in jurisprudence, by using the major rules, which are in his possession. They say that he is infallible and, therefore, he will not make mistakes while using analogy. They resorted to this argument because of the restrictions of their doctrine about the knowledge of the imām, who was not a mature adult, in their opinion.

Some of them said that the imām can be non-adult, even if his age is very young, because he is Allāh's witness, and it is possible for him to attain the knowledge even if he were a child. All the means [of miraculous learning] – such as inspiration, dreaming, the counseling angel, and other means – can be available for him, in the same way they were possible for his ancestors – the late witnesses of Allāh. They cited the example of Yaḥyā (John) b. Zakariyyā. Allāh gave him sound judgment from the time he was a child. (Qurʾān, 19:12) and ʿĪsā (Jesus) b. Maryam (Qurʾān, 19:24-33) and the child's judgment in the matter of Yūsuf (Joseph) b. Yaʿqūb (Jacob) and the king's wife (Qurʾān, 12:26-27) and the knowledge of Sulaymān (Solomon) b. Dāwūd (David) – the last two judged [correctly] without being taught, and many other examples. It is certain that some of the witnesses of Allāh were not adults in the eyes of people.

Muḥammad b. ʿAlī b. Mūsā, peace be upon him, was born in the middle of Ramaḍān 195 AH. Al-Muʿtaṣim[1], during his caliphate, summoned him to Baghdād, wherein he arrived two nights before the end of Muharram 220 AH. He died in the same year, in the end of Dhul-Qaʿdah; he was buried in the cemetery of Quraysh, near his grandfather Mūsā b. Jaʿfar, peace be upon him. His age was twenty-five years and two months and twenty days. His mother was a captive named al-Khayzurān and she was called "Durrah" before that. The duration of his imāmate was seventeen years. His followers, who continued to believe in his imāmate, went on to acknowledge the imāmate of his son, and heir, ʿAlī b. Muḥammad[2], and remained so. However, a few of them believed in the imāmate of his brother Mūsā b. Muḥammad[3] for a while, but converted thereafter to the belief in the imāmate of ʿAlī b. Muḥammad, peace be upon him. They rejected the imāmate of Mūsā b. Muḥammad until the death of ʿAlī

[1] Muḥammad al-Muʿtaṣim b. Hārūn al-Rashīd (d. 227 AH) was one of the strong ʿAbbāsid caliphs. He built Sāmarrāʾ (north of Baghdād) in 222 AH.

[2] ʿAlī al-Hādi (d. 254 AH) is the tenth imām of Twelver Shīʿa. The ʿAbbāsid caliph, al-Mutawakkil (d. 247 AH) summoned him from Medīna to Sāmarrāʾ to keep an eye on him. He remained there until he died. His shrine is visited until today.

[3] Mūsā b. Muḥammad al-Mubarqaʿ (d. 296 AH) was living in Kūfa and migrated to Qum, where he remained until his death.

b. Muḥammad, peace be upon him. His death was in Surra Man Raʾā (Sāmarrāʾ). Al-Mutawakkil[1] had previously brought him from Medīna with Yaḥyā b. Hirthima b. Aʿyun, three days before the end of Rajab 254 AH. He was forty years old when he died, and his arrival in Surra Man Raʾā was seven days before the end of Ramaḍān 233 AH. He was born on Tuesday, 13th of Rajab, 214 AH. He stayed in his home, in Surra Man Raʾā, for twenty years and nine months and ten days – until he died. The duration of his imāmate was thirty-three years and seven months and his mother was a captive named Sawsan – or Sumāna, according to some accounts.

The Numayrīyya

A sect from the believers in the imāmate of ʿAlī b. Muḥammad has deviated during his life by claiming the prophethood for a man named Muḥammad b. Nuṣayr al-Numayrī[2], who claimed to be a prophet and that Abū al-

---

[1] Jaʿfar al-Mutawakkil (d. 247 AH) was an extremist in his hatred for the family of ʿAlī b. Abī Ṭālib. He gave the order to demolish the grave of Imām al-Ḥusayn b. ʿAlī in Karbalāʾ. He was assassinated in a plot by his own son, al-Muntaṣir Billāh.

[2] He was a follower of Imām al-Ḥasan al-ʿAskarī, then he deviated and claimed the prophethood for himself (al-Kashshī, *Rijāl*, pp. 520-21). Al-Nuṣayriyya sect was named after him.

Ḥasan al-ʿAskarī[1] has sent him. He believed in metempsychosis and made extreme claims about Abū al-Ḥasan – saying that he is a god. He also permitted all the impermissible acts, including homosexuality among men – considering it part of humility and modesty, and claiming that it is one of the good pleasures and that Allāh has not prohibited any of them. This al-Numayrī was supported by Muḥammad b. Mūsā b. al-Ḥasan b. al-Furāt[2]. When he was terminally ill, his tongue became paralyzed. He told those who asked him about his heir that he designated Aḥmad. But it was unclear which Aḥmad he meant. His followers became divided into three sects. One sect said that he designated his own son, Aḥmad; and another sect said that he designated Aḥmad b. Mūsā b. al-Ḥasan b. al-Furāt; while the third sect said that he designated Aḥmad b. Abī al-Ḥusayn b. Muḥammad b. Muḥammad b. Bishr b. Zayd. They remained permanently divided, while these men claimed being prophets after Abū Muḥammad. These sects were called the Numayrīyya.

When ʿAlī b. Muḥammad b. ʿAlī b. Mūsā al-Riḍā, peace be upon them, died, one sect of his followers be-

---

[1] Al-Ḥasan al-ʿAskarī (d. 260 AH) is the eleventh Imām of the Twelver Shīʿa. He was called "al-ʿAskarī" because he lived in Sāmarrāʾ, which was built as a garrison. It was called "Madīnat al-ʿAskar (City of the Troops). He was buried in the same city, next to his father. His shrine is still visited by the Shīʿa.

[2] Muḥammad b. Mūsā b. al-Ḥasan b. al-Furāt (d. 254) was considered an extremist and a heretic. (Al-Kashshī, *Rijāl*, p. 521)

lieved in the imāmate of his son, Muḥammad[1], who died in Sāmarrāʾ (*Surra Man Raʾā*) during his father's life. They claimed that he did not die, citing that his father designated him for the imāmate after him, and that the imām is not allowed to lie. They also said that this is a matter about which Allāh would not change his will. Therefore, despite the appearance of his death, he did not really die. Indeed, his father was concerned about his safety, so he hid him. They claimed that he is al-Mahdī, which is a similar claim to that of the followers of Ismāʿīl b. Jaʿfar.

The rest of the followers of ʿAlī b. Muḥammad believed in the imāmate of al-Ḥasan b. ʿAlī, peace be upon him, and affirmed it according to his father's designation. He was called "Abū Muḥammad." However, a small circle followed his brother, Jaʿfar b. ʿAlī,[2] saying that his father designated him to be the imām after Muḥammad's death, and made his imāmate obligatory. They denied the imāmate of his brother Muḥammad – saying that his father pretended to exclude Jaʿfar for his protection, but he was indeed the imām.

Al-Ḥasan b. ʿAlī, peace be upon him, was born in Rabīʿ al-Thānī, 232 AH and he died in Sāmarrāʾ on Friday, the eighth of Rabīʿ al-Awwal, 260 AH. He was buried

---

[1] Muḥammad b. ʿAlī (d. 252 AH) is one of the esteemed members of family of the Prophet. His shrine is located in Balad, between Sāmarrāʾ and Baghdād, and it is being visited by the Shīʿa.

[2] Jaʿfar b. ʿAlī (d. 271 AH) was called al-Kadhdhāb (the Liar) because he claimed the imāmate for himself after his brother, al-Ḥasan al-ʿAskarī.

in his home, which is the same burial place as his father. He was twenty-eight years old. Abū ʿĪsā b. al-Mutawakkil[1] led the funeral prayer for his body. His imāmate was five years, eight months, and five days. He died without leaving an apparent son. Therefore, he was inherited by his brother, Jaʿfar and his mother – a captive nameed ʿUsfān and Abū al-Ḥasan then named her Ḥadīth.

[1] The son of the ʿAbbāsid caliph, al-Mutawakkil.

The Divergence After the Death of al-Ḥasan b. ʿAlī

His followers became fourteen[1] sects after his death. One sect said that al-Ḥasan b. ʿAlī is alive, but he disappeared and he is al-Mahdī, for it is impossible for him to die not leaving an acknowledged son; otherwise the world would remain without an imām. His imāmate has been established and it was also established from the Ḥadīth that al-Mahdī has two periods of occultation. This occultation is therefore one of them, then he will reappear and be known before he will disappear for a second time. They said about him what the Wāqifa said about Mūsā b. Jaʿfar. If they were asked, "What is the difference between you and the Wāqifa?" they would say that those Wāqifa were erroneous when they stopped at Mūsā, when his death was declared. He died leaving a successor, whom he designated [as an imām] – that was al-Riḍā, peace be upon him, in addition to more than eleven sons. So, every

[1] Al-Nawbakhtī mentions fourteen sects, but he provides descriptions for thirteen sects only. The fourteenth sect is reported from al-Sharīf al-Murtaḍā's book, *al-Fuṣūl al-Mukhtāra*, wherein a sect is reported as having claimed, "The Imam, after al-Ḥasan, is his son, Muḥammad, and he is the awaited one (*al-Muntaẓar*), but he died; he will return with the sword and will fill the earth with fairness and justice, as it was filled with oppression and injustice."

imām, who undoubtedly dies, in the same way his fathers died, and leaves a known successor, is dead without a doubt. But al-Mahdī – at whose life we are allowed to stop – is the one who dies without a successor. His Shīʿa are compelled to stop at him until he returns, because it is impossible for an imām to die without a successor. Therefore, it is true that he went into occultation.

The second sect said, "al-Ḥasan b. ʿAlī died and came to life after his death, and that he is al-Mahdī because we narrate that al-Qāʾim (al-Mahdī) is the one who rises after his death and that he has no son. But should he leave a son behind, then his death would be final, and the imāmate would belong to his successor. Since he did not designate any successor, then he is al-Qāʾim, for there is no doubt that al-Ḥasan b. ʿAlī undoubtedly died without leaving a son or designating a successor. Therefore he rose after his death. We also narrated that when the news of the rising of al-Qāʾim reaches people, they will wonder how he can be the imām after having been mere bones. Therefore, he is hiding now and will appear to lead the people and fill the world with justice, in the same way it was filled with oppression." They say that he rose after death and that he is in hiding because, according to them, the world cannot be without an [imām], either alive and recognizable, or hiding out of fear. They base that on the statement of ʿAlī b. Abī Ṭālib, peace be upon him, "O God! You will not deny the world an [imām], either recognizable or in hiding, so that your proofs and miracles will not fade away." This, they said, is the evidence for his rising after his death. Indeed there is no difference between this sect and the one mentioned before it, except that this sect acknowledged his death, whereas the other sect said that he disappeared and denied his death. This is also similar to the sect of the Wāqifa, who stopped at Mūsā b. Jaʿfar, peace be upon him. If they were asked, "Why did you say this? And what is your proof?" they would interpret the stories and some historical accounts.

The third sect said that al-Ḥasan b. ʿAlī died and the imām after him is his brother, Jaʿfar; and that he designated him for the imāmate. If they were told: "But they had never been on good terms throughout their life; and you have known about the acts of Jaʿfar and his mistreatment of his brother when he was alive, and his heirs, in dividing his inheritance," they would say that they only appeared so, but in reality, they were on good terms. Since Jaʿfar was always obedient to al-Ḥasan, and he appeared to be otherwise, then it must be at the orders of al-Ḥasan, for Jaʿfar was the heir of al-Ḥasan, who inherited the imāmate from him. They would cite the opinions of the Faṭḥīyyah, who said that Mūsā b. Jaʿfar became an imām because he was designated by his brother, ʿAbdullāh. Therefore, he received the imāmate from his brother – not from his father. They accepted the imāmate of ʿAbdullāh b. Jaʿfar after denying it for the sake of consistency of their doctrine. Their chief, who lured them to this belief, was a man from the theologians of Kūfa named ʿAlī b. Alṭāḥi al-Khazzāz. He was a famous member of the Faṭḥīyyah. He supported the imāmate of Jaʿfar and attracted people to him, for he was a skillful debater. He was aided in this task by the sister of al-Fāris b. Ḥātim b. Māhawayh al-Qizwīnī,[1] but she disputed the imāmate

[1] Al-Fāris b. Ḥātim al-Qizwīnī was considered a heretic. Al-Kashshī reports that Imām Abū al-Ḥasan al-ʿAskarī ordered his companion, Junayd, to kill al-Qizwīnī. (*Rijāl*, pp. 522-28)

of al-Ḥasan b. ʿAlī, peace be upon him, and said that Jaʿfar – not al-Ḥasan – was designated by his father.

The fourth sect said that the imām after al-Ḥasan was Jaʿfar, and that the imāmate was transferred to him by his father – not from his brother, Muḥammad, or from al-Ḥasan. They claimed that [Muḥammad] and al-Ḥasan were not imāms, because the former died during his father's life and the latter died without leaving progeny and he was fraudulent in his claim. Their evidence was that imāms do not die before designating their successors and leaving progeny, but al-Ḥasan died not leaving a successor or progeny. Therefore, his claim for the imāmate was erroneous. Also, the imāmate cannot belong to al-Ḥasan and Jaʿfar because of the statement of Abū ʿAbdullāh Jaʿfar b. Muḥammad and others from his fathers, peace be upon them, that the imāmate cannot belong to two brothers after al-Ḥasan and al-Ḥusayn, peace be upon them. This proves that the imāmate belonged to Jaʿfar, and that he received it from his father – not from his two brothers.

The fifth sect went back to the imāmate of Muḥammad b. ʿAlī, who died during his father's life. They said that al-Ḥasan and Jaʿfar claimed what did not belong to them, and that their father did not designate them for the imāmate; and no one attributed to him any hint of that which makes their imāmate obligatory. Besides, they were not qualified for it, especially Jaʿfar, who had blameworthy qualities that cannot be in a just imām. As for al-Ḥasan, he died without leaving progeny. This led us to believe that the imām was Muḥammad. He was certainly designated by his father, while al-Ḥasan died without leaving progeny – which is impossible for an imām – and we saw that Jaʿfar, during and after al-Ḥasan's life, had been impious and engaging in the disobedience [of God]. This would not make him worthy of testifying in a matter of a dirham's worth, let alone being worthy of occupying the position of the Prophet, peace be upon him, and his family. For Allāh, the Exalted, did not allow the testimony of an impious person, who declares his disobedience; how would he then honor him with the imāmate, which is highly treasured and much needed by the people? It is the means to knowing [Allāh's] religion, and the way to his satisfaction; how can it be allowed for a declared ungodly person? Since disobedience is not permissible, even for the *taqīyyah*, and to accept the imāmate of Jaʿfar is not likely to come from the Wise and the Exalted. When it was clear that Jaʿfar was not qualified for the imāmate, and that a man without progeny could not be an imām, we have no choice but to believe in the imāmate of Abū Jaʿfar Muḥammad b. ʿAlī, their brother. He was known for his piety and godliness and he had progeny, in addition to his father's designation of him. We can either believe in his imāmate and that he is al-Mahdī, or deny the imāmate altogether, which is not permissible.

The sixth sect said that al-Ḥasan b. ʿAlī had a son he named "Muḥammad"[1] and he declared him. Those who

[1] Muḥammad al-Mahdī (b. 255 AH) is the twelfth Imām of the Twelver Shīʿa. According to Shīʿite doctrine, he went into the Minor Occultation upon his father's death and remained in hiding for sixty-eight years. During this period, he remained in contact with his deputies. When the fourth deputy – ʿAlī b. Muḥammad Al-Samirī – died in 329 AH, the Imām went into

claim that he died without progeny were wrong. How would an imām, whose imāmate was established and was known for the elect, as well as the general public, die without progeny? Indeed, his son exists and he was born [several] years before his death. They did not doubt his imāmate and the death of al-Ḥasan, and that his name was Muḥammad. They claimed that he was hiding because he feared Jaʿfar and other enemies, and that it is one of his times of occultation. They said that he is the Imām al-Mahdī, and that he was known during his father's life, who designated him. Since his father had no other progeny, then he is the imām without doubt.

The seventh sect said that al-Ḥasan had a son, who was born eight months after his death, and those who claimed that he had a son during his life are lying and erroneous. For if that were true, he would not fear the others, but he died without leaving a son, that is known. It is unlikely that he would deny it and dispute what is obvious and reasonable and rational. The pregnancy was established and known to the authorities and the people, thus his inheritance was not divided until it [i.e. the pregnancy] was no longer established to the authority and was unknown. His son was born eight months after his death and he ordered that he be named "Muḥammad," who is in hiding. They supported their claim by a statement attributed to Abū al-Ḥasan al-Riḍā, peace be upon him, "You will be tested by the fetus in his mother's womb and by the infant."

---

the Greater Occultation. He will remain in hiding until he appears and overpowers all his opponents.

The eighth sect said, "al-Ḥasan had no son at all, because we have verified that and we have tried to establish it by all possible means, but were unable to establish his existence. For, if it were permissible for us to say that a man like al-Ḥasan – who died without a son – had a son, such claim could be said about any dead person without progeny. It would be even possible to claim that the Prophet, peace be upon him, and his family, had left a son, who is also a prophet."

The ninth sect said that al-Ḥasan b. ʿAlī was an imām whose death was established, and so was the death of his father and his forefathers, peace be upon them. In the same way that his death was true according to the authentic account, it was determined that there was no imām after al-Ḥasan. This, they said, is acceptable by reason and common sense. Like the prophethood was terminated after Muḥammad, peace be upon him, and his family, it is possible that the imāmate can be terminated. A statement was attributed to the two Ṣādiqs (al-Ṣādiq and al-Bāqir) that, "The earth cannot be without an imām unless Allāh, the Exalted, becomes angry with the people on earth because of their acts of disobedience; then he removes the imām until a certain time." This sect said, "Allāh, the Exalted, does what He wants, and our claim here does not cancel the imāmate. This is also possible according to another interpretation: there were no prophets or heirs of prophets between the Prophet, peace be upon him, and his family, and ʿĪsā, peace be upon him, (according to our narratives, there were periods of 200-300 years without prophets or heirs of prophets). In the same way, the earth today is also without an imām until Allāh wills to send al-Mahdī, a man from the family of Muḥammad, peace be upon him, and his family. He will revive the earth after its death, as He sent Muḥammad, peace be upon him, and his family, after a period of time to renew the religion of ʿĪsā and the previous prophets, peace be upon them. In this way, He will send al-Mahdī if He wills. Our authority, until his coming, is the permissions and prohibitions of the previous [imāms] and what has been attributed to them and become part of our body of knowledge, and our adherence to the deceased [imām], as we admit his death. In the same way, the source of authority for the people before the rise of our Prophet, peace be upon him, and his family, was the command of ʿĪsā, peace be upon him, and his prohibition and the knowledge attributed to him and his heirs. In addition to that, their obligation was accepting his prophethood and adhering to his heirs, while admitting his death.

The tenth sect said that Abū Jaʿfar b. ʿAlī, who died during his father's life was the imām. His father designated him by name and by person. They said that an imām, whose imāmate was authenticated, could not designate a non-imām. When Muḥammad died, he was not allowed to neglect the will and the designation of an imām. Of course, he could not designate his father, who inherited the imāmate from his own father. He also was not allowed to practice the imāmate (command and prohibit and appoint another who does that), because his imāmate was supposed to begin after the death of his father. Since he was not allowed to neglect the designation [of a successor], he designated a young servant of his father named Nafīs, whom he considered honest and trustworthy. He gave him the books, the knowledge, the weapons, and everything the people might need. He asked him to give all of that to his brother, Jaʿfar, when something happened to his father. He did not inform anyone about this, except for his father. He did that to remove any suspicion and to hide the matter. When Abū Jaʿfar died and the members of his household, who preferred Abū Muḥammad al-Ḥasan b. ʿAlī, knew about his story, they envied him and wanted to hurt him. Sensing what they had planned for him and fearing for his life – as well as for the imāmate – he called Jaʿfar and appointed him [an imām] and gave him the whole trust, which he received from his brother, Abū Jaʿfar Muḥammad b. ʿAlī, who died during his father's life. He did that as he had been ordered. The same thing was done by al-Ḥusayn b. ʿAlī b. Abī Ṭālib, peace be upon him, when he went to Kūfa. He gave his books, his will, his weapons, among other things to Umm Salama[1], the wife of the Prophet, peace be upon him, and his family. He trusted her with all that and ordered her to deliver everything to ʿAlī b. al-Ḥusayn al-Aṣghar, when he returns to Medina. When ʿAlī b. al-Ḥusayn returned from Syria to her, she delivered everything to him. This, therefore, is the equivalent of the imāmate for Jaʿfar, according to his designation by Nafīs, on behalf of his brother, Muḥammad. They denied the imāmate of al-Ḥasan, peace be upon him, saying that he was not designated by his father, who also did not change his appointment of Muḥammad, his son – which is an authentic account in their opinion. On this basis, they believed in the imāmate of Jaʿfar and debated with others

[1] Umm Salama (d. 62 AH) was the Prophet's wife. He married her in 4 AH, after the death of her husband. She is revered by all Muslims, especially the Shīʿa, because of her continuous support for Imām ʿAlī and his progeny. She transmitted 387 Ḥadīths from the Prophet.

about it. This sect forged many things about Abū Muḥammad al-Ḥasan b. ʿAlī, peace be upon him, and accused him and the believers in his imāmate of being blasphemers. They also exaggerate about Jaʿfar and call him al-Qāʾim. They prefer him over ʿAlī b. Abī Ṭālib, peace be upon him, and believe that al-Qāʾim is the best person after the Messenger of Allāh, peace be upon him, and his family. Nafīs was taken and thrown in a big basin in the house containing a lot of water. He drowned in it. This sect is called the Nafīsīyya.

The eleventh sect said, when asked about the imām, "We do not know what to say about this matter. It is not certain whether he is from al-Ḥasan's progeny or one of his brothers. However, we say that al-Ḥasan b. ʿAlī was an imām, who has died, and the world cannot remain without an imām. We say nothing further, until we verify the matter.

The twelfth sect (the Imāmīyya) said that all these sects were wrong. Indeed, Allāh, the Exalted, designated an imām from the progeny of al-Ḥasan b. ʿAlī, and Allāh's order is final. He is the heir of his father according to the established path and past tradition. For the imāmate cannot belong to two brothers after al-Ḥasan and al-Ḥusayn, peace be upon them. It cannot belong to other than the progeny of al-Ḥasan b. ʿAlī until the end of humanity, and it will continue in this way as long as the religion exists. If there remain two men, one of them must be al-Mahdī; and should one of them die, then al-Mahdī is the one remaining alive. Also, the imāmate cannot belong to the progeny of a person, who was not an undisputed imām and who died during his father's life. Otherwise, the claim and doctrine of the followers of Ismāʿīl b. Jaʿfar would be legitimate. Also, if this were true, the imāmate of Muḥammad b. Jaʿfar would be legitimate and his followers would be right when they made this claim after the death of Jaʿfar b. Muḥammad. They said, "What we say here is attributed to the two Ṣādiqs (i.e. al-Ṣādiq and al-Bāqir). These sects do not dispute it, because there is no doubt about its authenticity and rational basis. For the world cannot be without an imām, or it will not continue to exist. All other claims are baseless. We submit to the late [imām] and admit his imāmate, as we admit that he has a successor from his own progeny, who is the following imām until he appears and declares his imāmate as his forefathers did. It is up to Allāh to allow this to happen, for He is the final arbiter; He does what He wants and commands what He wills, be it his appearance of disappearance. As the Commander of the Faithful has said, 'O God! You will not deny the world an [imām], either recognizable or in hiding, so that your proofs and miracles will not fade away.' That is how we were ordered to believe, and what was said in the authentic statements of the imāms that were transmitted to us. For it is not up to the people to investigate Allāh's affairs and judge without true knowledge, or trace that which was not revealed to them. Also, it is not permissible to mention his name or ask about his location until he is ordered to [appear], because he, peace be upon him, is hiding, afraid, and veiled by Allāh's veil. We must not investigate his affairs, for it is forbidden. Indeed, revealing what was veiled will lead to shedding his blood and ours, which are protected by silence." They also said that it is not permissible for anyone of the faithful to choose an imām according to their opinion or according to elections. For Allāh designates him and He chooses him for us and makes him prevalent if He so wills, because He is more knowledgeable about what is better and more beneficial than His creatures are. The imām knows himself and his times better than we do, they continue to argue. Abū ʿAbdullāh al-Ṣādiq, peace be upon him, was a known imām and his location was made public and his lineage was visible and his reputation was known by the inner and outer circles. He said, "May Allāh curse anyone who refers to me by any name." That is why the men from his Shīʿa would meet him and turn away from him. It was said that a man from his Shīʿa met him in the road and turned away from him, without even greeting him. He thanked him for that and told him, "So-and-so met me and greeted me. He was wrong in doing that." Similar accounts were narrated about Abū Ibrāhīm, Mūsā b. Jaʿfar, peace be upon him, who forbade naming him in the same way. Abū al-Ḥasan, ʿAlī b. Mūsā al-Riḍā, peace be upon him, also said, "Had I known what they wanted from me, I would doom myself with breeding pigeons and fighting roosters and the like." How can this be permissible then in our own time of government oppression and disregard for their status? For, despite what [al-Ḥasan], peace be upon him, suffered at the hands of Ṣāliḥ b. Waṣīf[1], he did not mention him or declare his name or his birth. Furthermore, many accounts were transmitted to us, that al-Mahdī's birth would not be common knowledge and he would not be known. Nothing would be known about him, except that he will not rise until he appears and it

[1] Ṣāliḥ b. Waṣīf (d. 283 AH) was a ʿAbbāsid general of Turkish ancestry. His ruthless methods were unsuccessful with Imām al-Ḥasan al-ʿAskarī.

will be known that he is an imām and a son of an imām – an heir and a son of an heir (*waṣiy ibn waṣiy*). He would be a model [for certain people] before he rises. Yet, the inner circle of his father, and his own inner circle, know him, although they are small in number. The progeny of al-Ḥasan cannot be extinct from the earth as long as the affairs of Allāh, the Exalted, are on it. The imāmate cannot belong to the brothers and the hint and designation cannot be established without witnesses – at least two or more. This doctrine has been the path of establishing the imāmate – it is the doctrine, which the true Shīʿa hold.

The thirteenth sect followed the claims of their jurists and pious leaders, such as ʿAbdullāh b. Bukayr b. Aʿyan and his peers, who said that al-Ḥasan b. ʿAlī was the imām after his father and he died. They claimed that Jaʿfar b. ʿAlī was the imām after him, in the same way Mūsā b. Jaʿfar was an imām after ʿAbdullāh b. Jaʿfar, according to the transmitted account that, when the imām dies, the imāmate belongs to the oldest of his sons. However, they say, what was attributed to the imām al-Ṣādiq, that "the imāmate cannot belong to two brothers after al-Ḥasan and al-Ḥusayn" is true and obligatory, but only if the deceased has left progeny of his own. Then it would not be transmitted to his brother. It belongs to his progeny. However, if he dies without progeny, it necessarily transfers to his brother – which is the interpretation of the statement in their opinion. They also said that the body of the deceased imām could not be washed by a non-imām. This, according to them, is an authentic rule. They admitted, however, that Jaʿfar b. Muḥammad's body was washed by Mūsā, but they claimed that he did it at the instruction of ʿAbdullāh, and he [i.e. Mūsā] was the imām after him. They said that Mūsā was allowed to wash the body because he was the silent imām at the presence of ʿAbdullāh. This sect was the pure Faṭḥīyyah, who accept the transmission of the imāmate between two brothers, if the older brother does not leave a son. The imām according to them was Jaʿfar b. ʿAlī, because of the necessity, according to this interpretation and according to the narratives, which we already described.

Bibliography

Original Sources:

Al-Ash'arī, Abū al-Ḥasan. *Maqālāt al-Islāmiyyīn*, vols. I & II. Cairo, 1954.

Al-Baghdadi, Abd al-Qahir. *Al-Farq Bayn al-Firaq*, Cairo, 1964.

Al-Bāqillānī, Abū Bakr. *Kitāb al-Tamhīd*, Cairo: Dār al-Fikr al-'Arabī, 1989.

Ibn al-Athīr. *al-Kāmil fi al-Tārīkh*, vols. VII – VIII. Beirut, 1983.

Ibn Ḥazm, Ali b. Aîmad. *al-Faṣl bayn al-Milal wa al-Ahwā' wa al-Niḥal*, Cairo, 1964.

Ibn al-Jawzī. *al-Muntaẓam*, vols. VIII – IX. Beirut, 1995.

Ibn Kathīr. *Al-Bidāyah wa al-Nihāyah*, vols. XI – XII. Beirut, 1966.

Ibn Khaldūn. *Kitāb al-'Ibar wa Dīwān al-Mubtada' wa-l-Khabar*, vol. III. Beirut, 1957.

_____. *Muqaddimat Ibn Khaldūn*, Cairo: Mu'assasat al-Ḥalabī (n.d.).

Ibn Qutaybah, Abdullāh b. Muslim. *Al-Imāmah wa-l-Siyāsah*, Cairo: Mu'assasat al-Ḥalabī (n.d.).

Al-Ḥamawī, Yāqūt. *Mu'jam al-Buldān*, Beirut: Dār Iḥyā' al-Turāth al-'Arabī, 1979.

Al-Ḥillī, al-Ḥassan b. Yūsuf b. al-Muṭahhar. *Kashf al-Murād fī Sharḥ Tajrīd al-I'tiqād*. Qum (n.d.).

Al-Ḥusaynī, Ṣadr al-Dīn 'Ali b. Nāṣir. *Zubdat al-Tawārīkh*. Beirut, 1985.

Al-Ījī, Abd al-Raḥmān b. Aḥmad. *Kitāb al-Mawāqif*, vols. 1–3. Beirut, 1997.

Al-Isfarāyinī, Abu al-Muẓaffar. *Al-Tabṣīr fī al-Dīn*. Baghdād, 1955.

Al-Juwaynī, Imām al-Ḥaramayn. *Kitāb al-Irshād* (ed. Muḥammad Y. Mūsā), Cairo, 1950.

Al-Karājakī, Abu al-Fatḥ. *Kanz al-Fawā'id*. Beirut, 1985.

Al-Māzandarānī, Muhammed b. 'Ali Ibn Shahrāshūb. *Ma'ālim al-'Ulamā'*. Najaf, 1961.

Al-Mufīd, Muḥammad b. Muḥammad b. al-Nu'mān. *Awā'il al-Maqālāt*. Qum, 1951.

_____. *al-Fuṣūl al-'Asharah fī al-Ghaybah*. Beirut, 1993.

_____. *al-Fuṣūl al-Mukhtārah*, Beirut: Dār al-Mufīd, 1993.

_____. *Taṣḥīḥ al-I'tiqād*. Qum, 1951.

_____. *al-Nukāt fi Muqaddimāt al-Uṣūl* (n.d.).

_____. *al-Ikhtiṣāṣ*, Qum (n.d.).

_____. *al-Irshād*, vols. 1 & 2. Beirut, 1995.

_____. *al-Ifṣāḥ fi al-Imāmah*, Qum (n.d.).

_____. *al-Nuṣrah li Sayyid al-'Itrah fi Ḥarb al-Baṣrah*. Beirut, 2001.

_____. *Amālī al-Shaykh al-Mufīd*. Qum, 1982.

_____. *Mas'alah fi al-Irādah*. Qum (n.d.).

_____. *Tafḍīl Amīr al-Mu'minīn*. Qum, 1991.

_____. *'Adam Sahw al-Nabiyy*. Qum (n.d.).

_____. *Aḥkām al-Nisā'* (ed. Mahdī Najaf), Qum (n.d.).

_____. *Risālah fi Ma'nā al-Mawlā*, Qum (n.d.).

Al-Najāshī, Aḥmad b. 'Alī. *Rijāl al-Najāshī*, vols. I & II. Beirut, 1988.

Al-Nawbakhtī, al-Ḥassan b. Mūsā. *Firaq al-Shī'a*, (ed. by Muḥammad Sādiq Baḥr al-'ulūm). Najaf, 1959.

Al-Nisābūrī, Sa'īd b. Muḥammad. *Kitāb al-Masā'il fi al-khilāf bayn al-Baṣriyyīn wa al-Baghdādiyyīn*. Leiden: Brill, 1902.

Qāḍī 'Abd al-Jabbār. *Sharḥ al-Uṣūl al-Khamsah*, Cairo, 1965.

_____. *Firaq wa Ṭabaqāt al-Mu'tazila*. Cairo, 1972.

_____. *Al-Mughnī fi Abwāb al-Tawḥīd wa al-ʿAdl*, 20 vols. Ciaro (n.d.).

Al-Qummī, Ibn Bābawayh. *Risālat Iʿtiqādāt al-Imāmiyya*. Trans. A.A.A. Fayzee. Oxford, 1942.

The Qur'ān. Trans. by 'Abdullah Yusuf 'Ali. New York: Tahrike Tarsile Qur'an, Inc., 1995.

The Glorious Qur'an. Trans. by Mohammed M. Pickthall. New York: Tahrike Tarsile Qur'an, Inc., 2000.

The Qur'an. Trans. By ʿAli Quli Qara'i. London: ICAS Press, 2004.

Al-Sharīf al-Murtaḍā. *Al-Ghurar wa al-Durar* (*Amālī al-Murtaḍā*), vols. I & II. Cairo, 1954.

_____. *Kitāb Tanzīh al-Anbiyā'*. Najaf, 1960.

_____. *Rasā'il al-Sharīf al-Murtaḍā*, vols. II & III (edited by Sayyid Mahdi Rajā'ī). Qum, 1984.

_____. *al-Shāfī fi al-Imāmah*, Qum, 1983.

_____. *Masā'il al-Murtaḍā*. Beirut: Mu'assasat al-Balāgh, 2001.

_____. *Al-Masā'il al-Nāṣiriyyāt*, Tehran, 1997.

_____. *Al-Muqniʿ fī al-Ghaybah*, Beirut, 1991.

Al-Shushtarī, Nūrullāh. *Majālis al-Mu'minīn*. Tehran, 1955.

Al-Shahrastānī, *al-Milal wa al-Niḥal*, Cairo, 1968.

_____. *Nihāyat al-Iqdām fī 'Ilm al-Kalām*, (ed. and trans. by A. Guillaume), London, 1934.

Sibṭ b. al-Jawzī. *Mir'āt az-Zamān*. Beirut, 2001.

Al-Ṭabarī, Muḥammad b. Jarīr. *Tārīkh al-Ṭabarī*. Beirut: Mu'assasat al-A'lamī (n.d.).

Al-Ṭūsī, Abu Ja'far Muḥammed b. al-Ḥassan. *al-Fihrist*. Beirut, 1983.

_____. *al-Iqtiṣād*, Qum (n.d.).

_____. *Al-'Uddah fī al-Uṣūl*, Qum, 1994.

_____. *al-Rasā'il al-'Ashr*, Tehran (n.d.).

Secondary Sources:

Abdel Haleem, M. "Early Kalam", in S.H. Nasr and O. Leaman (eds.) *History of Islamic Philosophy*, London: Routledge, 1996.

Abu Bakr, Ibrahim. "Some Epistemological Issues in Shi'ism and Sunnism," *Hamdard Islamicus*, volume 24 No. 2 (2001), pp. 31-40.

Akhtar, Sayyid Wahid. "An Introduction to Imamiyyah Scholars: Major Shi'i Thinkers of the Fifth/Eleventh Century," *Al-Tawhid*, volume IV No. 4 (1407 A.H.).

Anawati, G. and Gardet, L. *Introduction à la théologie musulmane*, Paris, 1950.

Busse, Heribert. *Chalif und Grosskönig; die Buyiden im Iraq (945-1055)*. Beirut, 1969.

Farrūkh, ʿUmar. *Tarikh al-fikr al-'arabi ila ayyam Ibn Khaldun*, Beirut: Dār al-ʿIlm li-l-Malāyīn, 1979.

Goldziher, Ignaz. *Vorlesungen über den Islam* (trans. as *al-ʿaqīdah wa al-Sharīʿah fi-l-Islām* by M. Y. Mūsā, A. Abdulḥaqq and A. Ḥ. Abdulqādir), Cairo: Dār al-Kitāb al-Miṣrī, 1946.

_____. "'Kitab al-Irshad' by Al-Mufid," *Al-Serat*, volume 3 No. 3 (1977).

Iqbāl, ʿAbbās. *Khāndān-i Nawbakhtī*, Tehran, 1966.

Kadhim, Abbas. "The Mysterious Journey of Moses (Qur'an 18:60-82): Does It Refute or Confirm the Shīʿī Doctrine of *ʿiṣmah*?," *International Journal of Shīʿī Studies*, volume 2 No. 1 (2004), pp. 97-120.

Ayatollāh al-Khūʿī, Abū al-Qāsim. *Muʿjam Rijāl al-Ḥadīth*. Iran, 1992.

Kraemer, Joel. *Humanism and the Renaissance of Islam: The Cultural Revival During the Buyid Age*. Leiden and New York, 1992.

_____. *Les Schismes dans L'Islam*. Paris, 1965.

Lari, Sayyid Mujtaba Musavi. *Imamate and Leadership: Lessons on Islamic Doctrine, IV.* Translated from Persian by Dr. Hamid Algar. Qum, 1996.

Madelung, Wilferd. "Imamism and Mu'tazilite Theology," in *Religious Schools and Sects in Medieval Islam.* London: Variorum Reprints, 1985.

_____. "Al-Mufīd," *Encyclopedia of Islam*, vol. VII (1993), pp. 312-13.

Muhajarani, A. "Twelve-Imami Shi'ite Theological and Philosophical Thought," in S.H. Nasr and O. Leaman (eds.) *History of Islamic Philosophy*, London: Routledge, 1996.

Pasha, Mukhtār. *Kitāb al-Tawfīqāt al-Ilāhiyya* (A.H. – C.E. dates). Ed. by Muḥammad 'Umārah. Beirut, 1980.

Pavlin, J. "Sunni Kalam and Theological Controversies," in S.H. Nasr and O. Leaman (eds.) *History of Islamic Philosophy*, London: Routledge, 1996.

Reynolds, Gabriel Said. "The Rise and Fall of Qadi 'Abd al-Jabbar," *International Journal of Middle East Studies*, volume 37 No. 1 (2005), pp. 3-18.

Sabri, Simha. *Mouvements populaires à Bagdad à l'époque 'abbāsside, IXe – XIe Siècles.* Paris:), Maisonneuve, 1981.

Sachedina, Abdulaziz. *Islamic Messianism: The Idea of Mahdi in Twelver Shi'ism.* New York, 1981.

Sourdel, D. "Les Conceptions Imāmites au début du XIe siècle d'après le Shaykh al-Mufīd," in *Islamic Civilisation 950-1150*, ed. D. H. Richards. Oxford, 1973.

Watt, Montgomery W. *Free Will and Predestination in Early Islam*, Edinburgh: Edinburgh University Press, 1948.

_____. *Islamic Philosophy and Theology*, Edinburgh: Edinburgh University Press, 1962.

Wensinck, A. *The Muslim Creed*, Cambridge: Cambridge University Press, 1932.